MEETINGS

Meetings

A Reporter's Notebook

Jess Stearn

Health Communications, Inc.
Deerfield Beach, Florida

www.hci-online.com

Library of Congress Cataloging-in-Publication Data

Stearn, Jess.
  Meetings: a reporter's notebook / Jess Stearn.
      p.   cm.
    ISBN 1-55874-539-4 (hard cover)—ISBN 1-55874-500-9 (trade paper)
    I. Title.
PS3569.T338M44   1997   97-7988
920.073—dc21   CIP

Publisher: Health Communications, Inc.
              3201 S.W. 15th Street
              Deerfield Beach, Florida 33442-8190

Cover design by Lawna Patterson Oldfield
Cover photo ©PhotoDisc, 1997

Contents

Part One: The Reporter's Notebook

Part Two: Books and Mystics

Preface

I feel there is no such thing as an accidental meeting in a meaningful life. And all life is meaningful. Every meeting with significance exemplifies a synchronicity that brings people together for a certain purpose or end. People fall in love at sight, or form friendships, having a familiar and warm feeling of knowing each other. Either through some mental attunement, as an antenna reaches out, or in some vague genetic remembrance the animals have. Perhaps in the thrust of a group or racial memory. Or as a concept of past meetings that people in the East accept.

Our meetings may well determine our path in life. In personal and professional relationships, in the peace we find within ourselves, in the acceptance of what we know of ourselves through the eyes of others. I have been fortunate enough to meet people I will never forget—and who changed my life. So that like the crossed lives of many others it was never the same again.

JS

Prologue

I believe I have gotten something out of every meeting I ever had. I remember sitting with Henry J. Kaiser, the master shipbuilder, as he defended himself against charges of profiteering. He spoke without rancor.

"I could not be a Christian, and do what they accuse me of. As a Christian, I believe first in helping my fellow man." He didn't have to say any more. The Kaiser hospitals said it for him.

I met with Winthrop Rockefeller at his model ranch in Arkansas. He could have relaxed with his millions like any Rockefeller, but he chose to elevate the economy of a state second only to Mississippi on the poverty level. He was the first man to put an African-American in charge of a major ranch in Arkansas. Big Rock of Little Rock. He went on to become governor.

I learned from the humble, the cop who risked his life in turbulent waters to save a boy's dog and the firemen who ventured into a crumbling building to carry out a dozen of their own who perished in the fire.

I felt the fear in a 12-year-old white boy as he stood up for a black boy's right to play with the rest, taking on a school bully two years older and pounds heavier. There was nothing racial about it. That boy was his friend. The fight went on in the schoolyard for the length of the lunch hour. The white boy was bloody and bruised but unbowed. And his friend played.

Many of my meetings seemed far-fetched at the time. Probably none more confounding than my confrontation with Maya Perez, the Great Maya, who told me, when I was still a newspaperman, that I would write about the metaphysical when I didn't even know what it was. All of which eventually led to a meeting with a well-known psychic and publishing her unlikely prediction that President Kennedy would be assassinated in office.

PART ONE

The Reporter's Notebook

City Editor

As a boy I stood for hours and stared through a sidewalk window at the roaring presses and imagined what it would be like to be a reporter on this newspaper.

I saw myself flying off to all manner of crimes and disasters, bringing back my story to a grateful city editor. I pictured what he looked like, and the staff of assistants and reporters. I had no idea what the City Room was really like, but I had seen it so often in my mind that I knew every nook and cranny, and every face. And I knew I would be working there one day.

Nevertheless, it was with some trepidation that I entered the City Room of that same paper years later, looking for my first job as a reporter. As I looked around the room bustling with people, my nervousness left me. I had been there many times. The room was as I had pictured it. Two large desks facing each other dominated the room. A volatile-looking man with a mop of curly hair was snapping out orders, the stodgy-looking man sitting across from him, nodding, and picking up a phone. Battered desks were banked around the room, and the rewrite men with their ears glued to headphones were

3

jotting down a note or two. Reporters were dashing around. It was deadline time.

Everybody was much too busy to notice the wide-eyed stranger, or I might never have gotten as far as I had. At this point, while I was considering my next move, the man with the curly hair looked up. His eye caught mine, and he motioned to an empty chair.

I sat down and marveled as he pulled together the threads of a fast-breaking news story. Then he looked across the desk at his assistant with a grunt of satisfaction, and turned to me.

"You're quite young," he said, before I could explain myself.

"I can't help that," I said.

He laughed. "You're not what I expected."

His phone rang. He picked it up. As he listened, a frown darkened his face for a moment and he said, "No harm done. Good luck."

He was still frowning as he put down the phone and gave me an appraising look. "So who the hell are you?" He pointed to the phone. "That was the guy coming in for an interview."

"Whatever it is," I said, "I can handle it."

The assistant city editor looked across the desk with a grin. "He certainly got in here all right. How did you do it, kid?"

I shrugged, not too sure of myself. "I just walked in like it was home."

The curly-haired man scowled. "How did you know I was the city editor?"

I took a deep breath, and glanced around the City Room. It was quieter now with the edition put to bed. A dozen reporters and rewrite men were sitting around their desks, smoking and chatting. They looked just as I had visualized them, and so did the youthful-looking city editor staring at me out of narrowed eyes. How could I tell this man that I had already visualized myself getting the job, not even knowing there was one open?

"You just looked like a city editor," I said, thinking how inane the words sounded even as I said them.

He gave me a hard look. "What experience do you have?"

What experience could I possibly have just out of college? I had worked on the college newspaper for two years, and the humor magazine for three years. It didn't sound like very much.

"As much experience," I said, "as Jack London or Hemingway before they got their first job."

He sat back in his chair and laughed. It was a booming laugh that seemed to bounce off the walls.

"Okay, Hemingway, when can you start?"

The Ceiling

Whatever else about Curly, he was not a bigot. He couldn't care less what a man's pedigree was. But he did like tweaking a man's nose when he thought he was stuffy and self-righteous. He had nicknamed stout John, his assistant city editor, the bishop, because of his staunch Catholicism. And the nickname had stuck, with even John taking a secret delight in it.

There was nothing pompous about John. He had just missed his calling. He was a good newspaperman, but he would have made a better priest. He had a feeling about people that kept him from rising to the top. It was a compassion that always had him feeling sorry for the rogues of the world, when all he should have been thinking of was exposing them. He let too many bad guys slip through his fingers, and lost too many stories. That is why they put him on the desk. But somehow I had the idea that he never minded any of this. I think he had only one deep and abiding regret. Given the opportunity to do it all over again, I have an idea John would have stayed in the seminary and gone on to be a monsignor.

That is why I felt he would have given his right arm for the assignment Curly was giving me. In fact, when Curly called me over, John raised his big body out of his chair, and came around the city desk to hear better what Curly had to say.

Curly handed me a slip of paper with a name and address on it, and gave me a wink that John couldn't miss. He liked teasing John but he respected him, or he wouldn't have had him sitting across from him.

"Listen, kid," Curly said, "this being Good Friday, we're getting a lot of crank calls about spirits dropping out of the sky, and turning up on people's ceilings. Take a photographer, Louie Raczkowski, if he's clear, and find out what these mackerel-snappers are so worked up about."

I had never heard the expression before. But from the pained look on John's face it wasn't difficult to guess who Curly was talking about.

I'd never seen John so interested in a story. He put an arm around my shoulder, leading me a step at a time away from Curly's amused smile.

"Don't take your cue from Curly. If true, this is a very solemn event. It would mean an awful lot to a lot of people."

"Thanks, John, I'll remember that."

I looked up to catch Curly's eye. I could see he hadn't missed a thing. He was the city editor of our small town newspaper, the best city editor I ever knew, and a demanding boss. I knew I would have to come back with something.

I picked up Louie in the darkroom, and off we went. It was about a 20-minute drive. Louie was a few years older than I, dark and intense, and proud of his Polish ancestry. He liked to talk about how the Poles had beaten the German knights in battle 500 years ago. I didn't mind his running on like this because it gave me a chance to think about my assignment.

I was a little concerned because I knew that people took religion, especially their own, very seriously. I didn't want to step on any toes but I knew I would have to report what I saw and what I heard, if there was anything to it at all. I knew how important it was to people because my own belief in God was important to me. There wouldn't be any miracles unless He made them happen. I didn't see anybody else making miracles, not by a long shot.

I was glad Curly had given me Louie as my photographer. He was young enough not to flaunt his seniority and uneducated enough not to patronize me with his superior knowledge. It was a standoff. Louie didn't know anything about reporting and I didn't know anything about taking pictures. It didn't seem like anything special to me. All the pictures the photographers took looked pretty much alike when they got into the paper, dull, flat and gray.

It had been raining off and on for days, and nobody knew if it would ever let up. I didn't think there would be much of a crowd. Though the sun showed signs of breaking through the clouds, there was still enough of a drizzle to dampen anybody's ardor.

Louie drove with one hand and talked with the other. He was as happy as a clam to be on this assignment. He took a silver chain off his neck and held in his hand a medallion that was the likeness of a robed woman. The Madonna. There was a red heart over the robe just where the heart should be.

"This," he said, "is what you're going to see."

I looked at him in surprise. "So when were you there?"

He put the medallion back around his neck.

"Last night, on my own time."

We drove on a while, and soon began to break into the ragged edges of a crowd. I was amazed as we went on to see the lines of people standing in the rain. There must have been close to 3,000 people. A few wore raincoats, but most, oblivious of the rain, were in sweaters or jackets. They were the quietest crowd I had ever seen. The three or four mounted police on duty had little to do but sit their horses. They saw our press card on the windshield and waved us through. We were almost to the house before we had to stop because of the crowd which had overflowed into the street. We got out of the car and I helped Louie unload his equipment. He had brought a couple of extra cameras and enough film to cover the Battle of the Bulge. As he began taking his pictures outside the house, I sized up the people in line, talking to some as they slowly moved forward. There were men, women and children of various persuasions. Some of the younger people carried babies strapped around their shoulders. There were older people hobbling along with canes or crutches. There was no shoving, no ducking in line, no complaining. The younger people gave way to the older, and the older smiled their acknowledgment. I had seen a light in Louie's eye when he touched his medallion. I saw the same light in the faces of the crowd edging closer to the house which had become the center of interest. I watched an elderly couple, in their late seventies or eighties, wiping the fine rain from their faces.

"How long have you been in line?" I asked.

"Oh, two or three hours, I guess." The man looked to his wife for assurance. "Oh, yes," she said, "but we don't mind."

At that moment the sun came out and a huge rainbow drew a spectacular arch across a clearing sky. Hundreds of faces turned heavenward, and there was a spontaneous cheer as if this were a signal from above. As I studied the crowd it dawned on me that these people saw themselves as pilgrims on their way to a holy shrine. However their emotions varied, the experience they were sharing drew them together. Not all were Catholics. There were Protestants, some Jews, and atheists moved by a perverse curiosity. Even the lovebirds were there. I saw a young couple clinging to one another. The young man would bend down and kiss the mist off the girl's tousled hair and she would kiss his hand and give him a look that had the radiance of the morning sun.

I stopped for a moment.

"What brings you here?" I said.

They gave me a warm smile.

"We're Christians," the young man said, "we believe in Christ and the Second Coming. All the people of the world need help right now. And if that image on the ceiling is what they say, it could be a sign that God is sending us a message."

The thought wasn't that well constructed but I knew what he meant. If the Mother showed her face, the Son wouldn't be far behind. And God would be looking over their shoulders. It was a nice thought.

I was almost to the house now and I could see Louie on the porch, shading his eyes.

"What took you so long?" he demanded. "I've been waiting an hour."

I looked at my watch.

"All right," he said, "a half hour."

Armed with a camera, Louie became a new and bolder warrior. With a couple of cameras slung over his shoulders, he pushed his way through the crowd into a room teeming with people. I noticed two priests standing in a corner, talking to a man and woman of middle years who were smiling deferentially. Every once in a while, the couple would turn and motion to the room beyond. I assumed that was the room where we would find what we were looking for.

The priests, I thought, were there to examine the ceiling with a clinical eye, and proclaim a miracle which would inspire the faithful wherever they were.

"How about a picture of the priests talking with that couple? It must be their house."

Louie nodded. "Yeah, they were here last night. How about the ceiling?"

"That'll wait. The priests won't."

As we approached, the priests broke off their conversation.

"Would you pose for a moment with our host and hostess?"

The woman giggled nervously. "I must do something with my hair. I'll be back in a moment."

The older of the two priests looked at me and shook his head. "We prefer no publicity."

I looked at him in surprise.

"Even if it's a miracle?"

"We are exploring that possibility, young man. But even if the figure has been miraculously conceived and is that of the Mother of our Lord, it will be years before evidence can be marshaled for the approval of the Holy Father in Rome."

Our hostess had returned, looking little different than she had before. Her face fell as the priests backed off and we took a picture of her and her husband by themselves. But her aplomb soon returned when I suggested a picture of her pointing at the ceiling in the adjoining room.

The Flanagans were modest people. This was the big event of their lives. Smiling, they led us through the throng into the shrine room. The furniture had been removed and the room was jammed with humanity. The scene reminded me of what I had heard of shrines in other lands. As they lifted their eyes to the ceiling, some of the women cried out, and crossed themselves, bursting into spasms of sobbing. Others fell to their knees and broke into fervent prayer. In the crush, I saw a young woman, shaken by tremors, falter and collapse. She was raised up by two guards and carried into a bedroom. The men appeared to react differently, loathe to show emotion.

Two or three of the taller men reached up on tiptoe, but couldn't quite reach the ceiling. It was as if they were trying to make something tangible of what they saw by touching it.

Raising my eyes, I had my first glimpse of what I had come to see. It was a dark silhouette on a white plastered ceiling. Jostled as I was, I had to crane my neck. Even so, examining it closely, I could see where it resembled Louie's medallion. It was oval in shape, some eighteen inches long and three or four inches wide. It was as if somebody had retraced Louie's medal in dark and somber shades. Even the halo about the head was similar, and the heart a deeper shade which made it stand out. There was an expression of composure, a placidity, the serenity of a mother with a son chosen of God.

So engrossed was I that I didn't realize for a moment that somebody was trying to gain my attention. It was our hostess, Mrs. Flanagan. She whispered in my ear, "Nothing was there two or three days ago. It began to form yesterday and took its present shape only this morning, Good Friday."

Louie had positioned himself for a classic picture.

"Can I see your medal again?" I said.

Grudgingly almost, he took it off and handed it to me. In every detail it corresponded with the image on the ceiling. It was almost too good a likeness. I considered the alternatives. It would have been easy to have faked the whole thing. All the Flanagans had to do was fill in the figure from a transparency they could have purchased anywhere and who would have known? What had they to gain? It was all too apparent. All one had to do was look around the house and down the street and see the celebrity they had achieved. Their modest little lives were already invested with a new importance.

I kept looking at the figure, trying to arrive at a plausible explanation. A small circle had been cleared to give Louie room to shoot. As he was focusing I moved about, looking at

the figure from every angle. The thought had occurred to me
that the rain dripping in from the roof might through some
odd chance have formed this unique pattern on the plastered
ceiling. It was a long shot but it was possible. I had seen ceilings leak through in my grandmother's home. They usually
left meaningless splotches in the plaster. Sometimes, though,
a vague body or head.

I had a feeling there was more to the image than met the
eye, but I had no idea what it was. I wasn't to be kept in the
dark long. At this point, as I was looking at the figure, something occurred that almost made me jump out of my skin.
The figure suddenly became alive. Before my very eyes it
appeared to pulsate, its tone and texture changed. It grew
darker and seemed to fill out, there was a clearer definition.

I rubbed my eyes in disbelief. I was aware of a gasp next to
me, and I saw Mrs. Flanagan sink slowly to her knees, cross
herself, and begin praying. Louie's eyes had widened and his
dark face paled as if he had seen a ghost. He stood transfixed,
unable to take a picture.

I didn't know what to make of it. But as the movement in
the figure stopped, I saw Mr. Flanagan standing nearby, and
motioned to him. He came over, and followed my pointing
finger.

"Do you notice anything different?" I said, trying to keep
my voice casual.

"No, it looks like the same Holy Mother to me."

His wife gave him a cross look. "Lawrence, don't be dense.
Of course, there's a difference. Don't you see how much more
alive it is?"

She had dusted off her knees, and looked transformed. She
was almost attractive.

I nodded at the ceiling. "Is there a crawl space over that
spot?"

Flanagan shrugged, "Nothing but the roof. Look for yourself."

I measured the distance to the ceiling with my eye, making a mental note to measure that distance against the roof height as we left.

I looked out the window. The rain had stopped and I was glad of that. It always rained heavily about this time of the year and there was nothing anybody could do but think how it made the trees and flowers grow. There was a good side to everything, even if you didn't always see it right away.

I stopped outside, and looked up at the roof. There was no way anybody could have crawled between the shingles and the ceiling, unless it was a snake, and I couldn't see a snake doing silhouettes.

It had been a great day for Louie. He collected his equipment and with his cameras slung over his shoulders strode through the crowd into the street. The lines were still long, stretching out as far as we could see. The news of a miracle was spreading, though there had not been a word in a newspaper or on the airwaves.

Louie and I rode in silence, thinking our separate thoughts.

"Well?" he said finally, giving me a sidelong glance.

"I don't know. I can't make up my mind."

He scowled and lapsed into a disgruntled silence. I could see he didn't like my lack of enthusiasm, but he wasn't a reporter with a story to write. All he had to do was take pictures.

Not another word was spoken till we got to the Chronicle parking lot.

"How many pictures are you printing?"

He looked at me as if I was an outsider.

"I dunno. Maybe a dozen." He slipped out of the car with his cameras. "Maybe they'll use a couple of pictures, maybe not. It's no big deal."

I had not taken any notes because of the downpour, and the crowd in the house, but I remembered everything, the expression of the people, every line and shadow of the dark figure that had a life of its own.

Curly looked up as I walked into the City Room.

"Ah," he said, "the hunter home from the hills."

He swiveled his chair around and faced me. John had moved his chair around the big desk so he wouldn't miss anything.

"Well," said Curly, with a look for John. "Let's hear all about the great miracle."

With this one statement he managed to put me on the defensive. I didn't know enough then to know how to handle it. It made me overcompensate a little. I mentioned the crowd and how it had impressed me.

"It was a moving demonstration of a people's yearning for a spiritual experience."

"Never mind that. What did you see?"

"They were like pilgrims visiting a holy shrine."

He gave me a bleak look.

"Stop editorializing. What about this vision? That's what you were sent to investigate."

I could see John smiling, giving me an encouraging look.

I was trying to show how it affected people. I thought it important, for it said something about a people's dream. But maybe Curly knew all that. He had been around a lot longer, and knew more than I did.

I gulped but I got it out.

"It was an excellent likeness of the Immaculate Heart of Mary. I don't see how it could have looked any more like the medallion itself."

His face took on an expression of infinite disgust. "What do you mean it looks like the Immaculate Heart of Mary? Are you saying it's a miracle when the Catholic Church says it isn't?"

I was about to say I wasn't saying anything of the kind when John held up a protesting hand. "Hold on, Curly, I told you the monsignor called and said they couldn't say what it was or wasn't at this time."

"If it wasn't, then it isn't," said Curly. "Let's stop the doubletalk."

His voice softened a little. He had made his point.

"Tell me why you think it's the Lady."

"I didn't say that. I just said it looked like her."

"They could have stuck a ladder into the room one night, and smudged the silhouette onto the wall. Didn't you consider that?"

I was irked. He wasn't giving me credit for a grain of intelligence. "That was the first thing I considered. But I ruled it out."

He shot up in his chair.

"Why?"

"Because before my very eyes, and those of a dozen others, including the photographer, the silhouette changed its tone and texture. It became a moving, living thing."

Curly's eyes widened in mock wonder.

"Where did you and that photographer stop off?"

"I didn't have a drop, nor did Louie."

John had opened his mouth, but Curly cut him off.

"I want it from our bright young reporter."

I took a deep breath. "Here's what I think, based on what I saw. The rainy season begins just before Easter in our neck of the woods, and the rains come down hard and steadily. After a few days the water soaks through the roofs of many homes and seeps through the plaster ceilings. Sometimes it forms shadows that look like objects or places, like you see in the moon on a clear night."

Curly made an offensive noise with his puckered lips.

"Never mind the moon, stick to the ceiling."

"All I'm saying is that in this case, the water almost miraculously formed a likeness of the Lady of the medal. Yet for every silhouette with some shape or form, there must be thousands of meaningless splotches."

He nodded. "You're thinking straight now. No miracle, but a phenomenon born of the rain? Do I understand you correctly?"

I hesitated, seeing John's frown. "Yes," I said, "that became clear when the picture changed as we looked at it. It was a natural happening. A seepage from an over-accumulation of rainfall."

Curly swung his chair around with a triumphant smile.

"Now what do you think of that, Father John?"

There was a look in John's eyes I hadn't seen before. It was a distant look that seemed to travel beyond the room. He got up from his chair, and turned to leave, pausing in the doorway. There was no disappointment in his face, only that strange look in his eyes. His gaze rested for a long moment on Curly. Their eyes locked.

"Yes," said John, with the sweetest of smiles, "it was the rain, as you say. But who made it rain?"

Grandma

When we were young, my grandmother was always saying things like, "Your body is the temple of your soul. Always remember." Or, "You are only poor when you think you are."

They didn't sound very wise to me. I was 12 years old, and had an idea I knew more about the outside world than Grandma, who stayed in the house much of the time and darned clothes and made the meals. And had neighbors over for a spot of tea and homemade cookies. Yet she had ways of doing things that were kind of surprising, like joining a hospital auxiliary and helping the sick and invalided when she was so busy at home.

We never knew what was driving her. Or what she might do next. One day school was excused early and I came home for lunch. I found the young colored man who brought our ice sitting down at the kitchen table while my grandmother was serving him a big plate of meatloaf and mashed potatoes. It was cheap and filling and we had it quite often because there was a depression.

I don't know why, but it struck me as kind of odd that my

Grandma should be waiting on the man who brought the ice for our icebox. I laughed. Not a funny laugh. More out of surprise, I guess.

My grandmother poured some tea, then said in a quiet voice, "We have to be very caring with Austin. He just lost his wife, and we must let him know any way we can that we share his loss. And care about him."

I found myself flushing without knowing why. Austin had been listening with a faint smile on his face. "He's only a boy."

"Yes," she said. "But he will be a man one day and I want him to remember that we are all the same before the God who made us."

I always remembered.

The Chancellor

I slipped unannounced into the chancellor's office. He was sitting at his desk with a musing look in his eye and a rare smile on his lips. He looked up for a moment and frowned, as though I had caught him off guard.

He liked seeing me. I was a whiff of fresh air from the outside world. And as a recent graduate, part of his university. One to be trusted.

He was the first chancellor in memory who hadn't been a bishop and he had a common touch behind the austere exterior which I as a student had known something about.

His eyes lighted up behind their steel-rimmed glasses as he said:

"Did you see the rabbi as you came in?"

I shook my head. "I came by the side door."

I had never seen him so moved. Not when I was a student, and not as a reporter. The gray of his face had become suffused with color. There was a glow I had not seen before. There was something he had to get out, I could see that. And he did, speaking in a quiet composed voice, so much like himself.

"I had not met the rabbi before. He called and asked if he could come in and chat after lunch. I had no idea what he wanted. I said I would be happy to receive him."

The chancellor liked what he saw. A middle-aged man with a serious look and yet a smile that bespoke of sensitivity and humor. He seemed uncomfortable at first, as though uncertain of how to come to grips with what was on his mind.

The chancellor sought to put him at ease.

"Tell me, rabbi, is there anything I can do for you?"

The rabbi's face brightened. "As a matter of fact there is," he smiled. "I have a concern for the Jewish students at the university."

The chancellor was the head of a Methodist-oriented university. He sat up in his chair.

"And what is this concern?"

"When Jewish students observe their holidays, the Jewish Passover and the Day of Atonement, Yom Kippur, they are penalized for class cuts. On the other hand, when Christian students observe the Christmas and Easter holidays, there are no cuts."

I had been listening with interest, knowing that unwarranted class cuts could limit student privileges and even lead to expulsion.

"And so what did you tell the rabbi?"

The chancellor smiled.

"I told him there were no Christian or Jewish students at the university. There were only students. I explained that what he called the Christmas holiday was our midyear school break and the Easter holiday the spring break."

His eyes met the rabbi's.

"All students," he said, "are alike in my eyes."

The rabbi rose from his chair and there were tears in his eyes. "Chancellor," he said, "this is what my people have been wanting to hear for 5,000 years. I thank you, and I know my people will thank you."

He shook the chancellor's hand and left, with a new spring in his step.

The chancellor sat back in his chair. He had the same reflective look in his eye as when I walked in. For a moment I didn't exist. He was alone with his thoughts. I looked at this venerable figure, who so seldom revealed any emotion, and saw the suspicion of a tear behind the steel-rimmed glasses.

"It is a story I would like to use, sir."

"Some day," he said.

Sandburg

"You haven't been around," Curly said, taking me aside. "So you have no idea of the trouble brewing on the paper."

"You mean about the union?"

He gave me a jaundiced look. "So they've gotten to you."

"One of the guys mentioned it. He said it wouldn't help me with management. But something to think about."

His eyes circled the City Room, taking in a gaggle of reporters and rewrite men. He had a dark look. "It's for the big city papers. They're impersonal. This is your hometown paper. Nothing to worry about. So long as you do your job."

He smiled. "Which reminds me. I got a cushy assignment for you. Carl Sandburg."

"Carl Sandburg. He wrote all those books on Lincoln. Casey Jones. And the fog comes in on little cat feet."

Curly threw his feet up on the desk. "The appointment's all set. Just knock on his hotel door."

He nodded as I turned away. "Now remember. You came here to work. Not negotiate. Get moving!"

I kept moving. Mr. Sandburg was reading a newspaper when I knocked. He put it aside.

Standing, I saw how long and lanky he was, and wrinkled, with a gaunt face and gentle eyes. Like Mr. Lincoln.

I had scribbled some questions walking over to the hotel. We never took a cab when we could walk. Not on our home-town paper. I stuffed the questions in my pocket.

He leaned back in a love seat, poking at the newspaper. "I worked on that sheet in Chicago. Still think like a newspaperman. A noble profession." He gave me a second look. "You're pretty young."

I'd heard that before. I nodded, trying to think of something professional. Without success.

"I like newspaper people." He gave me an approving eye. "I try to help. Walked many a picket line."

I looked at my watch. He could only give me a half-hour. Ten minutes were gone.

I thought about his books about the great emancipator. The prairie years and the war years. Thick, heavy volumes rich in detail. A brilliant portrayal of Lincoln's progress from the farmlands of Kentucky and Indiana to the Illinois lawyer years and his ascension to the presidency. And martyrdom.

They had common roots in Illinois. I thought this may have had something to do with Sandburg's interest.

"What got you writing about Abraham Lincoln?"

His mind from the look on his face appeared to be miles away.

"Oh, that. I was brought up on Lincoln." He frowned. "I understand the newspaper guild is having a hard time in your community."

I sat back in surprise. "I'm new on the paper."

"Yes. Raw clay, ready to be molded."

I was getting uneasy. The half-hour was nearly up. And I

didn't know any more about Sandburg, or Lincoln, than I did before.

"What," I injected, "was the secret of Mr. Lincoln's greatness?"

"He loved people. The people on the farms and factories and the battlefield. The people of the South and the North. Government of the people, by the people, for the people."

This was a little better. The Gettysburg Address.

I slipped in another question. "How would he handle our problems today?"

"A good question. He stood strong for labor. The right to strike. The first president. I'm sure he'd tell you to join the union."

He stood up with a smile. The interview was over. I walked back to the newspaper wondering what I would say to Curly. My hand dropped in my pocket. I'd completely forgotten my questions.

"Well," said Curly, rolling back in his chair. "What have you got?"

I braced myself. "Nothing much. Pretty general. Lincoln's principles. That kind of thing."

"There had to be more. With all those books. What else?"

His voice was hard and demanding.

I lowered my voice. No more than a whisper.

"He told me to join the union."

The Vanishing Doctor

*H*e was a mild-mannered man with pink cheeks and gray hair. Who could have been lost in a crowd. He was softspoken. With a twinkle in the bright blue eyes. He looked like he would have been perfectly happy sitting on the front porch sifting through a small-town weekly.

And yet I had been told that he was the outstanding physician in the country. The doctor who had put Johns Hopkins Medical Center on the map. His name was Howard Kelly.

"To what," I said, "do you owe your distinction as a doctor?"

He smiled. "Oh, I'm not all that sure about my distinction."

I was a cub reporter. But I knew this man must be different, have done something special. For the medical center connected with his name had achieved a worldwide reputation second to none. And he had done it.

I thought of other doctors I had talked to. Boasting of the 30 or 40 patients they saw every day, planting them in little cubbyholes, getting them out before the chair got warm. He didn't look or talk like any of them.

I could see him considering me with a kindly eye. Patient.

And the least bit amused. Probably wishing he was on that porch with his newspaper.

"You must have introduced some new approach to medicine? Some new way of treating the sick? A new remedy?"

"It's really nothing to get stirred up about. Just something I tell young doctors. And I do myself."

I leaned forward.

He noted my new interest. His eyes twinkled even more brightly.

"I listen to the patient. I have no better source. No one has better insight into a patient. He has been living with himself a long time."

I thought of the assembly-line doctors and their cubbyholes. Dashing from one patient to another. An eye on the clock. Barely knowing the name of the patient. Or remembering the ailment without checking a pad.

"Doesn't listening take some time?"

"Oh, yes, but it may save a life. And that's what it's all about."

Jawn

I remember him standing off in Tim's one day and wrinkling his nose at the throngs clamoring to get at the bar. He had only himself to blame. He had made an "in" place of this crusty old bar with his *New Yorker* tales of the Irish saloon-keepers who quoted Shakespeare and Shaw and traded barbs with Steinbeck and Hemingway.

"Nobody comes to Tim's anymore," Jawn said with a mournful wag of his head. "It's too crowded."

I saw Jawn infrequently after he left the paper, and invariably it was at the spa he had made famous. I ran into him there, in an off-hour, the day I was assigned to do a story on Jim Thurber, author of *The Secret Life of Walter Mitty* and celebrated cartoonist. Thought by some to be our leading humorist. His was no ordinary story. He had accomplished so much while being blind, with the help of the woman he called his seeing-eye wife. Now by a cruel twist of fate her eyesight was being threatened. And they would be left in darkness. Surgery was her only hope. What must be going through Jim's mind, and his wife's? How was he standing up to this new stroke of misfortune? As a writer with no visible handicap, who had done so little, I marveled how he had done so much without eyes. He was truly a marvel.

I tried to reach him. It was impossible. He could not talk to me. He could not talk to anybody. He was devastated. He was in a hospital room next to hers, praying.

I mentioned all this to Jawn as we sat in Tim's. I saw him look up at one of Jim's cartoons tattooed on Tim's walls. He smiled. It was a sad smile, and yet there was a sweetness, as if some recollection went along with it.

"Do you know him?" I said.

He smiled. "Almost since I can remember. We worked on the same paper together back in Ohio when we were growing up." He gave a rueful laugh. *"The Columbus Dispatch.* We called it The Disgrace."

I didn't ask him to help me. I didn't have to. He knew the Thurber story inside out. He thought it needed telling.

"I have never known a man," he said, "whose good luck and bad luck are so tied in together. Every time he has some good fortune, it seems to be followed by a stroke of misfortune. His first play, *The Male Animal,* clicks and Jim makes his first big money. And then less than a year later he loses his sight. He adjusts with the help of his wife. Then what happens? His wife's sight goes bad. That's the way it's always been with Jim, good and bad. It's remarkable the way he stands up under it. It goes back to his childhood. When Jim was six years old his brother accidentally shot out Jim's left eye with a toy arrow. The incident was never mentioned between the brothers. I have an idea Jim developed his compassion for people feeling sorry for his brother. He never let it interfere with his work. Despite warnings from the doctors he built a brilliant career, writing and drawing, taxing the one good eye. He was an inveterate reader before his eyesight failed him. Five operations couldn't bring it back, and this may haunt him when he thinks of the affliction that struck his wife, and the surgery she faces. But he always lives in hope. There is no other way he could have beaten Lady Luck."

Jawn told me only what he thought Jim would have told me had he been able to. He knew Jim wouldn't mind. For he had no intention of belaboring Jim's bad luck. He knew Jim would want him to be upbeat.

"The good Lord provided Jim with a helpmate who became his eyes. With her at his side, he kept in touch with movies and television. He could follow them by listening. When there was no sound his wife would describe the action to him.

"She was his editor, chief critic, proofreader. She read to him by the hour from newspapers, magazines and books. Only a few days before she went into the hospital, she finished checking the draft of a book which was a collection of his short pieces. Only she could read his unreadable hand.

"He would scrawl giant-size letters with a soft black pencil on yellow copy paper. He would have a thousand words framed in his mind before he started getting it down. He would put 20 words on a sheet. When he finished a short story it was about the size of a novel.

"All this on the work side helped Jim maintain his balance. He lost himself in his work. But without his wife it would have been meaningless. She was his tower of strength. She sustained him with her faith. And now he's helping her with the strength he drew from her. It is a great love story. In all those years of blindness he never saw his blindness as anything but a challenge because of her. She was his consciousness and he hers. They were in total harmony.

"They would make something special of whatever they did. She got to picking out his clothes. All of a sudden he was the best-dressed humorist in town. He would make a joke of it and say she had such good taste that he never saw a tie she picked out that he didn't like.

"I remember his saying being blind was an advantage in writing. He used to say he couldn't write in this room or that. With his sight gone every room became like every other room. He didn't find his eyes wandering to watch a bird or a pretty girl. Blindness made him dig deeper into himself, and into other people.

"He had a photographic memory. He could remember word for word, even to punctuation, short stories he had written weeks before. But he was no slave to facts. As a reporter, when the phones began jangling on the city desk, he'd quietly reach for his hat and steal out of the office.

"But just tell him about some violets growing on the side of a hill in the winter, and he'd come up with a heartwarming story of a little girl plucking violets in the snow with her near-frozen fingers, and taking them to some sick old man who was so heartened by this kindness that he would respond by getting well. Jim was always upbeat. If he were here with us he'd say, 'Don't write anything that will alarm anybody. We both know everything will be all right.'

"Sing no sad songs for Jim," said Jawn, with the faintest suggestion of a dewy eye. "Nobody knows better that brave men look life in the eye and laugh, with it or at it. That's what Jim has been doing all his life."

It was Jawn's story not mine. I was embarrassed by the compliments. But he had pledged me to silence. "Anybody can talk a story," he said, "you put it on paper."

Jim Thurber called a day or two after the story was in the paper. He was full of optimism for his wife's recovery, and grateful for a story about himself that he could listen to without wincing.

"I don't know who you talked to," he chuckled, "but I have a pretty good idea. He knows me as well as I know myself."

Some time passed before I saw Jawn again. I heard of him often, though. He was commuting between Hollywood and the Big Apple. He had married well, and his wife was keeping him on an even keel. He was writing for the movies, and for the book publishers and the magazines. He was drinking some, but seemed to have it under control. Then months passed, without my seeing anything he had written or hearing about him. He was not seen at any of his old haunts, not even Tim's. I could understand that, for, as he said, the place was too crowded. As for Jim, his wife's eyesight appeared to have been helped. I think Jawn must have helped it with his thoughts.

Not much was happening to me. I worked for the newspaper in one department then another, liking the change. Then one day the editor told me they were setting up a special feature department.

"Don't get any ideas you'll be the star," he said. "We have a number of luminaries we're bringing in to beef up the paper. You'll be one cog in the machine."

They had thrown up a lot of partitions, with big glass windows, so that it looked more like an insurance office than a newspaper. I had a desk on the end with a clear view of the wall. I was beginning to think they were trying to tell me something, but maybe not.

"Be there at nine in the morning," the editor said. "I want you to meet some of the new people. I think you'll be pleasantly surprised."

His sly smile said anything but that.

I was there at nine, and a few minutes after the hour who should shuffle in but a man I would have least expected. I could hardly believe my eyes. It was Old Jawn himself. He sort of shambled in, with a shamefaced smile, and extended a hand that shook a little. His eyes were not as clear as I remembered them, and some of the color had left his face.

"What are you doing here?" I exclaimed in wonder.

He fidgeted about for a moment or so, then slumped into the chair I pulled up for him. He seemed very unsure of himself. He spoke almost apologetically.

"I thought I'd go back to work here until I straightened myself out. My wife thinks it's a good idea for me to get some discipline back in my life."

I could see that he had been having a difficult time. He looked haggard and drawn, and he kept running his tongue over his lips. The drinkers' complaint. Dry as a whistle.

I thought of all the wonderful writing he had done since he left the paper. All the marvelous elves and pixies he had created, all the wisdom he had expounded in the process. I couldn't bear the thought of some mediocrity saying, "Jawn, will you make a tour of the delis on the East Side, and see why turkey is selling better than ham?" Or something silly like that. I owed Jawn one. For Jim and his wife and the story he had given me. And for a lot more.

I had never asked a fellow newspaperman this question. I did it now with an apology.

"Forgive me, Jawn," I said, "but what will they be paying you?"

He frowned.

"Not much. That's not the idea. I got to get chained to a desk somewhere, get up a certain time and go home a certain time." He smiled wanly. "Or maybe I won't have a home."

So that was it. John had come to grips with old Demon Rum and the devil in the bottle had got the better of him. The old demon was a demanding master. He saw that his disciples did little more than worship at his shrine, until they were his completely. I recognized the symptoms. I had seen them all too often, without having to travel very far.

An idea had formed in my head. I repeated my question.

"Jawn, what are they paying you?"

He swallowed a few times, and looked away, before coming out with it. I could see why. It was a pittance, less than I received. They knew of John's plight.

I pursued my idea.

"Jawn, didn't you have a desk at *The New Yorker?*"

He nodded. "Quite a while ago."

"Do you remember what they paid you?"

He thought for a moment, his eyes squinting. I could see he was beginning to perspire.

"Oh, several times as much."

"Then why don't you go back?"

He looked at me uncertainly. "Do you think they would have me?"

"Have you? They'd love you to death."

We looked at each other, thinking our separate thoughts.

"It's not the money, Jawn. It's the not going backwards. It's like Jim and his wife. You said it so well. They looked life in the face, and they laughed at it. If Jim could go on, you can go on. You have eyes, Jawn. And the gift of laughter."

He stood up and took a deep breath.

"What shall I tell the editor?"

"I'll tell him, Jawn. I won't mind at all."

I could see the mist in his eyes.

"You really think I can do it?"

I thought of Jawn's great hero, Eamon de Valera, the aging leader of the Irish Republic, who told his critics:

"Whenever I need to know what my people want, I look into my own heart."

"Look into your heart, John," I said, "and you'll find all that you need." I gave him an embrace. "There aren't many like you. Know that, dear Jawn."

He moved off, putting on his hat, like the gentleman he was. I saw his shoulders go back and a new spring come into his step. All I could think of, as I stood in the hall, and watched his figure recede, was the Irish blessing he had given so many times:

> *May the road rise to meet you.*
> *May the wind be always at your back.*
> *May the sun shine warm upon your face;*
> *And, until we meet again,*
> *May God hold you in the palm of His hand.*

The Goddess

*G*race Kelly smiled as she told her story. It was late afternoon on a sweltering August day in Manhattan. She had been making the rounds for what seemed an eternity. Her feet dragged. And her arms ached from carrying the portfolio of pictures that hardly anyone wanted to see. Tall, gaunt, emaciated models were in vogue. And a fresh-faced blonde with the look of a Greek goddess was out. She was tired and discouraged. She'd been told, as she went from one audition to another, that she was too short, too petite, too wholesome looking. Not luminous enough, the photographers said, whatever that meant.

She'd heard it so often she was beginning to believe it. She decided to call it a day. Looking for a place where she could rest for a few moments, she spotted a small Russian restaurant on a Manhattan side street. There were only a few people in the place. A waiter, with an appreciative glance, brought her a pot of hot tea. As she looked up she was conscious of a middle-aged woman at a nearby table staring at her. The woman was dark and looked foreign. And somehow mysterious. She smiled as her eyes met the clear blue eyes of the younger woman. She came over and sat next to her. And introduced herself. "I am Rava. I am a sensitive. I can look into the future. I pick up on things. As you walked in I saw that you were discouraged. But you do not have to worry. For you will be world-famous one day."

Rava came with the restaurant. It was her boast that she was never wrong. "Never."

"I was amused," Grace recalled over lunch, "but it was the first encouraging word I'd had in months. So I sat back and listened. I was hard-pressed to get a modeling job and she was telling me I was to become Hollywood's brightest star. It was enough to make me laugh my tears away."

"Anyone might have said that just looking at you," I interposed skeptically.

"Well, nobody else did. Besides she was very specific in her predictions. She named all the top stars I was to star with. Gary Cooper, Clark Gable, Jimmy Stewart, Bing Crosby, Frank Sinatra, even Ray Milland, an English actor I was friendly with."

The thought had struck her that the tearoom psychic could have been angling for a substantial tip, but this was soon disposed of. "She refused to take any money from me. She said it wasn't very often she saw a future like mine. She predicted I would be back to share it with her. And I did." She frowned a moment, hesitating.

"There was another prediction. It was preposterous."

I marveled that she could have so little recognition of her own beauty. She said she was seldom noticed in the street. And rarely drew glances from passing males.

I could hardly believe it. "They must have been blind."

"No, it's true. I have a small face." She usually wore a hat over her lustrous blonde hair, which covered her eyes. She might as well have worn a mask.

The psychic's message had some impact. For she started thinking Hollywood. Her uncle, George Kelly, a well-known playwright, opened a few doors, but she did the rest. As they say in Hollywood, the camera loved her. The face she thought small filled the big screen, and magnified the perfect profile.

The moving camera picked up high spots that eluded the fashion photographer's meager lens: The crystal-clear blue eyes so wonderfully innocent and yet artlessly seductive, the exquisite radiance and vivid coloring. She could have played a princess without looking at the script. Her auditions were so good she started at the top. Her maiden effort was with Gary Cooper in *High Noon.*

She smiled, thinking back. So far the Manhattan seeress was on the mark. It was a Western. Grace photographed like a cowboy's dream. She did everything right. But something went wrong in the making and the picture didn't jell. There were unfavorable reactions from preview audiences. The picture was withdrawn and put on the shelf. The test audiences responded to her fresh beauty and subtle sex appeal. But now she was just another morning glory in the Hollywood graveyard. Rava's boast of a perfect record was nothing more. A boast. Gary Cooper washed his hands of the picture, which he had taken on with high hopes. But he had a kind word for Grace. "She remembered her lines and did everything right."

An unsung hero in production never lost confidence. He spent long lonely hours re-editing the film, prevailing on a grumpy Cooper to come down to the studio and view the revised version. Cooper saw it through, amazed. It was suspenseful. It worked. And Grace came through like a dream. It opened with the bad men riding in to the beat of ominous music to take over a town. Closeups of Grace were dug up and a new star was born. She had magic, the critics decided. A girl in a cowtown who looked like she had walked out of a fairy tale. The studios fought for her and so did the top stars. Clark Gable in *Mogambo*; Jimmy Stewart, *Rear Window*; Cary Grant, *To Catch a Thief*; Bing Crosby with Frank Sinatra in *High Society*; and the English star Ray Milland in *Dial M for Murder*.

"It was all like Rava said. She named each one of the actors I co-starred with. It was uncanny."

And that one prediction Grace had hesitated over? "Well, as I said, it was preposterous. She said I would marry a prince one day."

It was not all that absurd. For she looked more like a princess than any princess who was around. A year or so later, unexpectedly, she met Prince Rainier of Monaco and married him after a whirlwind courtship, announcing she was giving up her career.

But her interest in the psychic was renewed. Having looked into the mystic Edgar Cayce, who seemed to have an infinite knowledge of events, she played the Ouija board with a visiting actor and a palace friend. The Ouija board, citing Cayce, spelled out an invasion entailing three continents— Europe, Asia and Africa. England, France and Israel joined to wrest control of the Suez Canal from Egypt. The incident took place later that year and was aborted by President Eisenhower's intervention. As predicted.

Word of the Princess Grace's communication with spirits raced through the palace like wildfire, reaching the palace priest. Grace was told it was contrary to Catholic teaching to dally with spirits. She agreed to abstain. But her interest in the metaphysical remained strong. Some years later she visited Brazil to investigate reports of psychic healings with the aid of nuns in a Catholic hospital. On her flight back to Monaco she stopped off in New York City to attend a ceremony honoring the memory of her playwright uncle. There she got to chatting with Susan Strasberg, who was accepting an award honoring her late father, the dramatic coach Lee Strasberg, who had tutored Marlon Brando and Marilyn Monroe. My name came up and Grace told Susan, a mutual friend, to let me know of her visit to Brazil and her intention to sponsor such healings in the Monaco hospital. She was injured in an automobile accident with her daughter before she could get her project going. Hospitalized after the accident, on the critical list, she had more concern for her daughter who was relatively unhurt. She was a princess in every way.

The Addams Family

Charles and I had some sort of bond. There was something about his life that was as lugubrious and mordant as the cartoons that brought a smile and a laugh to the American public. Yet when I listened to him I felt only his pain and loneliness.

He had a good marriage when he was young and a lovely wife. There was one misfortune. This wife he was devoted to could not have a child. She wanted to adopt, having the normal maternal instincts. Charles hesitated. He was afraid of what the Fates might deliver. Always the pessimist. And so he wavered while his wife's need grew as her patience thinned.

Finally, he gave in, in a fashion to be expected of a Charles Addams character.

"He'll have to be at least 16."

This was not the baby a young mother wanted. She left him, and he grieved.

I would see him intermittently. *The New Yorker* crowd and the newspaper crowd didn't mix that much. One day, sometime thereafter, I popped into Tim's pub on Third Avenue for a fast lunch at the bar. Charles was just beginning to ease his long body off a barstool when I sat down next to him.

"I'll keep you company," he said, waving for another cup of coffee.

He looked even gloomier than the last time I'd seen him. "How's it going?" I said.

"Oh, so, so," he sighed. "I just don't seem to be able to get my life together. The only kick I get is working, and you can't work all the time."

I nodded sympathetically.

"I guess you're lonely. You know scads of people. Why don't you go out more? Get away from the job for a while. Don't even think about it."

He gave me a Charles Addams frown that was more of a scowl. "I've tried all that. It doesn't work. Nothing works."

I sighed to myself, thinking how he should have adopted, and everything would have been all right.

"Have you thought of getting married again? That might do something for you, raising a family, and all that. At least, you'll never be lonely with a flock of kids crawling all over you."

Even as I said this I was thinking what a wonderful Charles Addams cartoon it would make.

He shook his head and his eyes held the look of a basset hound that had just been reproved.

"I'm married," he said. "I got married a few months ago. To a lawyer."

I almost slid off my barstool.

I could think of little else to say.

"Good luck, Charles," I said. "Give me a call if you've got nothing better."

He must have gotten a divorce. For I saw his name linked in the columns with vintage movie stars like Joan Fontaine and Greta Garbo.

I happened to be thinking about him as I browsed through a shop at 50th Street and Madison Avenue. The thought being the father of the action, we almost collided as I stepped out into the street. He seemed glad to see me, almost breaking into a smile.

"I'm pleased that you've finally connected with somebody you like."

He looked at me questioningly.

I mentioned Garbo. It seemed an incredible match. The silent but aging Swede and the taciturn moody lampooner of the American scene.

He looked almost wistful.

"I missed on that one," he said. "I met her at a party, and mentioned I was planning to motor across the continent in a few days. She seemed to light up, and said how delightful it would be to do something like that."

He primped his lips and groused. "It never occurred to me until later that she would have liked to join me."

"That's the trouble with you, Charles. You don't appreciate yourself."

We had been standing in the midst of heavy midtown Manhattan street traffic, gradually sidling over to the curb.

"How about Joan Fontaine?" I said. "I remember her from movies as a real beauty with a nice way about her."

"Joan Fontaine?" His head shot back for a moment. "Where did you get that?"

"In the gossip columns. Where I get all my information."

He let out a sigh, shaking his head. "Joan Fontaine. She's too much for me. A great woman, but too much." His eyes had a haunted look. And then I saw his jaw drop. He was peering over my shoulder as though he'd seen a ghost.

I turned and saw a smiling Joan Fontaine. Standing a few feet away in a city of 8 million. She had eyes only for him.

"You'll have to excuse me, Charles," I said. "I'm running late."

I left him with a frozen look on his face. A look that only a Charles Addams could have properly caricatured.

I gave a party. It was for a lady that Charles dated occasionally, as a free and disengaged male.

It was a party small enough for communication. Most of the company were connected with magazines and books, and Charles fit in well. I checked him from time to time, wanting to make sure he was enjoying himself. He seemed preoccupied with a number of people, so at least he wasn't bored.

I had been planning to take a plane in the morning. I had let this be known, hoping for an early evening. By midnight most of the crowd had drifted off. A few lingered, but departed as I looked at my watch and yawned.

It was now four a.m. Only one guest remained. Charles. He had a drink in his hand, and was quite sober. I never knew him to be anything but sober no matter how much or little he drank. He sat down next to me, looked around the empty room, and said in a confidential whisper:

"You know a party never gets good until you're down to the hard core. That's what makes a party. The hard core."

I gave him a second look. I could see he was serious and sober. "Charles," I said, "we are the hard core. You and me. Everybody has left."

He smiled, or as close to a smile as he came.

"That's good," he said. "Now we can enjoy the party."

Note: Charles married a third time. It eased his loneliness. When he died memorial services were held in the New York Public Library. He was surrounded by thousands of friends—books.

No Smoking Please

I'd just come off the graveyard shift. It was two a.m. The bars had closed early. I was dying for a cigarette. I smoked two or three packs a day, having picked up the habit as a young reporter in the big city. It was a filthy habit. I'd quit a hundred times. I chewed gum till my jaws ached. I tried the water cure, tracking over to the drinking fountain till my legs ached. I read books on breaking bad habits and willpower. Nothing worked. Not for more than two or three days. I didn't keep cigarettes around the flat. One way of cutting down, and now I was bedeviled by my own restraint. The corner drugstore slammed a steel gate in my face and the bartenders pointed at the clock as they locked their doors.

Like the alcoholic in *The Lost Weekend* I trudged down a Greenwich Village street to my cheerless apartment. The street was deserted. There was nobody I could cadge a cigarette from. And then in the somber street light I spotted a lone figure shambling toward me.

I soon saw he was a denizen of the Bowery, the Skid Row refuge of the homeless who had no place to sleep but dark hallways and alleys. In the lamplight I made out the mottled cheeks and the spongy red nose of an aging man who drank too much. I shuddered at the sores on his lips, and the bleary eyes crusted with pus. The grime of the streets was etched in his skin and the stench of human excrement lay heavy on his soiled clothing.

He had a determined look and I had no doubt he was about to make a touch. As he opened his mouth I could see ridges of broken teeth black with decay. He had a hoarse wheedling voice and a clumsy bow that was meant to be ingratiating.

"How about an arf dollar for a pint of Dago Red, guv'nor?"

I flinched at his foul breath. But my craving for tobacco overcame my sense of smell.

"I'll trade you for a cigarette."

His face brightened in a gargoylish smile.

"Righto, guv'nor."

I gave him some change, and he rummaged into his filthy jacket. His hands were red and puffy, covered with the same sores I saw on his face. He pulled out a small pouch of tobacco and a tissue of cigarette paper.

"Don't you have a cigarette?"

"The finest smoking tobaccy." He smiled, displaying his rotting teeth.

To my horror, he licked the cigarette paper with his tongue, then filled it with tobacco, twisting the ends together so none of the precious weed would be lost.

"There ye be, guv'nor. Finest smoke you'll ever have."

My eyes passed over the sores on his face and hands, the crusty eyelids, the black teeth, the clothes that smelled to the high heavens. And I took the cigarette from his outstretched hand. Gingerly.

I struck a match, lit the moist end of the cigarette with difficulty, put it in my mouth. And inhaled deeply till I felt my tension ease.

"Always glad to help a young fella, guv'nor," he said as he toddled off.

I finished the cigarette as I climbed the steps to my second-floor flat. Stamping out the butt before I turned the key and opened the door. And then suddenly it hit me. I threw off my clothes and jumped into the shower, scrubbing myself furiously with antiseptic soap and scalding water. I brushed my teeth for 10 minutes, then rinsed my mouth with mouthwash. I thought of all the strange and malignant diseases I could get. And began itching all over my body. After a restless night I awoke with a picture of that salivating tongue passing over the cigarette paper I had put in my mouth. I brushed my teeth for another 10 minutes, vowing I would never smoke again. It was easy. All I had to do was conjure up a likeness of that ulcerated face and the grimy and scabietic hands, and my desire for a cigarette vanished. I didn't realize it at the time, but I was putting to good use the power of the visualizing mind I was to write about later in a book called *The Power of Alpha Thinking*.

The Vacation

Little Eddie was a Broadway press agent with more clients than he knew what to do with. He'd operated on the fringes of Times Square for 20 years without having a vacation. He lived, breathed and talked the Great White Way. I don't think he'd ever seen a blade of grass or a cow who wasn't on the cover of a can. He loved the hustle and bustle of his street. He rubbed elbows with the con men and the panhandlers, the pimps and the parasites. He knew the greats and the near-greats. It was nothing to see a Marilyn Monroe or a Marlon Brando lounging around his living room, dangling their feet over a fishpond the size of a washbowl.

The conversation at Eddie's was always animated, as though cranked up by the racket in the street outside. The honking of horns, the shouts and wild cries, the grinding of trucks and the grating noise of the trash men all clattering against the windows of his second-story walkup. I found his place an oasis amid the bedlam of Broadway. But wearing if you got too much of it, I decided, noticing Eddie's thin face beginning to look pale and peaked. The light, and the enthusiasm, had left the once sparkling eyes, listless now behind their tinted glasses. He had the look of a man on the way to a breakdown.

"You need a rest from all this," I told him. "Fresh air and fresh food, away from the people who haunt your place. Get out with the cows and the corn."

His clients agreed. "I got just the place for you," said his singing comedian as the garbage collectors noisily hauled away the load of trash from the sidewalk of the restaurant next door. "I'm driving you to a place in the mountains by a lake, with real animals and birds and fish." He eyed Eddie's little fishpond with disgust. "Not those piddling goldfish gurgling in that little sewer of yours."

Eddie sighed. "Maybe you guys are right," he said in a tired voice. "Maybe I need a change." He breathed a waft of diesel fumes from the open window into his thin chest. "Yes," he said with a bright smile, "fresh air and the birds chirping on the windowsill. Like in a movie."

He called that night. He was leaving in the morning. There was a wistful note in his voice.

"Who," he said, "will feed the goldfish?"

"Just go, and don't call till you get back. Stay away from the telephone. Everything is taken care of."

I kind of missed Eddie and his place. But it pleased me to think he was getting what he needed. A lot of fresh air and sunshine and, above all, the quiet of the great outdoors.

Three days after Eddie's departure I got an unexpected call. From Eddie.

My voice was reproachful.

"I told you not to call till you got back."

"I'm back," he said.

"You're back? You must be crazy."

"I couldn't sleep. It was those birds. They kept me up three nights in a row with their damn chirping."

A Driver a Month

I looked at the thick safety window separating driver from passenger.

"That's no protection," he said. "Not from a Magnum. We lose a driver a month. Driving a cab ain't no health farm."

"So why do you do it?"

He flashed his teeth in an amused grin. "I got two boys. Thirteen and fourteen. I want something better for them. I drive seven days a week so they have the right kind of home."

He frowned into the rearview mirror. And I saw a little sigh escape him.

"Soon enough I'll be losing them. So I do what I can now."

"What do you mean by that?"

"By the time they're in high school lots of black kids find out their daddies ain't the big guys they thought. They can't do anything for them. I can't help my boys get a job. Or get in a college. I wouldn't know where to start."

It was a revelation, something many whites didn't even dream about. "It's amazing," I said, "how little we know about each other. Even a reporter who's paid to know what's going on."

He smiled. "I guess it works both ways."

We had developed a good rapport by the time we got to Brooklyn. He had asked me a number of questions about what a reporter's life was like, and I had laughed and said, "I'm still trying to find out."

He had laughed along with me. "It still beats cabs."

I looked at the safety window and agreed.

As I got out of the cab and paid the fare, he gave me a half-wistful look.

"Do you think my oldest boy could get a job on a newspaper when he gets out of high school?"

I gave him a card. "Call me," I said. "Maybe you won't lose your boy when he's out of school."

The Tea Taster

"This man," the editor said, "was the tea taster for the last Empress of China."

I was 24 then.

"He must be a million years old."

He was an Englishman and he lived in Brooklyn in a hotel overlooking the harbor. There had been a snowstorm and the buses weren't running from lower Manhattan over the Brooklyn Bridge. Nor was any other vehicle. I decided to walk it. I was frozen by the time I got to the man's hotel. My lips wouldn't move, and my tongue was stuck to the roof of my mouth. Tiny icicles had formed on my eyelashes.

I pressed an elevator button for the top floor, and knocked on a door. It opened an inch or two, and a reedy voice inquired: "Who may this be?"

I said I was the reporter keeping my appointment.

The door opened slowly, and a little old man with a wizened face and a toque on his head made me a bow.

"Enter the abode of the last tea taster for the Empress of China."

Despite my youth, the various joints that moved my arms and legs were still stiff from the cold. "Ah," he said, ushering me to a chair, "a cup or two of hot tea is just what you need."

Tins, bags and boxes of Chinese tea were scattered all over the cluttered apartment with its wide-ranging view of the harbor and the Statue of Liberty.

He paraded all kinds of teas before my defrosting eyes. All with Chinese symbols on the packages. Orange teas, lemon teas, pekoes, unblended and blended, even an Earl Grey, which sounded more English than Chinese to me, until he explained that the blend was brought back from the Orient by the second Earl Grey, a British envoy to China.

He had stirred himself now, preparing a special blend favored by the empress.

"Did you know her?" I asked.

"Very well. We spent many an hour tasting these teas together. Deciding which blends were best for the world market. She had an exquisite taste. Infallible."

"And this is her favorite tea? I am honored." I was beginning to thaw by now, appreciating the warmth of the room. Watching with interest as he put one teaspoonful of tea in each pot.

"As you saw I warmed the pots first. It makes all the difference. Bringing out the delicate fragrance of the blend. A very heartening drink on a cold, windy day."

He gave me a kindly smile and his pale blue eyes lit up. "You were a brave young man to foot it over the bridge in the storm. I must make it up to you."

Disregarding my protests he put several tins of the Empress's favorite in a bag for me. "For the people in your office," he said. He was a gracious gentleman. "The empress would be proud."

By this time, the water on his little burner was whistling hot, and my body was aching for a cup of the promised tea.

The cup was boiling hot as he served it on a platter with the gold crest of the empress. He sat down opposite me, and offered a tray of cookies. I shook my head.

"I want nothing to distract from the taste of the empress's tea."

He gave me a benign smile. I could see that his bird-like eyes were watching me closely as I lifted the cup to my lips.

He had not exaggerated. There was an ambrosial fragrance to this royal blend.

I savored its taste, letting its warmth trickle for a moment over my tongue. It was hot, so hot I swished it around in my mouth for a few seconds, before swallowing. I felt my insides warm immediately, and the stiffness leave my joints. An involuntary smile came to my lips.

He looked at me with an approving eye.

"You like it?" he said, with the look of a spaniel wanting a pat on the head.

"Like it?" I said. "I love it. I feel like a new man. What a marvelous tea. I feel stimulated. Energized. I'll have no trouble walking back over the bridge. I've never felt so good, thanks to you and the Empress of China."

His lips parted in a grin revealing his stained teeth.

"It's the hot water," he said, rubbing his hands. "It does it every time."

The King

You had an idea whatever he did on the screen he could do in real life. He was the kind of man you'd want to go fishing with or have on your side in a tight squeeze. They called him "the King." It was a Hollywood publicity blurb, but I had an idea he fit the role a lot better than most of the royalty that had sat on thrones.

I began my research for my newspaper by watching re-runs of his old pictures. There was one I liked particularly, his greatest role, in the greatest picture ever made—Rhett Butler in *Gone with the Wind*. I thought I might see something in it I hadn't seen before. He was superb. I wondered how he had missed getting the Oscar for his performance. I found myself sitting there, empathizing, not thinking for a moment I was watching an actor. And yet it was thought he was not a great actor, not in the same class with an Olivier or Spencer Tracy. Still, scads of women, typifying the millions, would put on fresh nylons and Chanel No. 5 whenever they went to one of his movies. It was like they were having a date with the King.

I watched a dozen of his pictures, some good, some not so good, but he was always impressive. Always himself. This bothered me with other actors, but I liked it in him.

He had filmed a picture in Africa, which was a remake of a film he had done 20 years before. It was a whopping success at the box office. The two women he had played against in the original version were long out of movies. One was dead, the other an old woman. Two beautiful young stars, Ava Gardner and Grace Kelly, chosen in their stead. But the King was still playing the same he-man role, as irresistible as ever, and as believable.

As it happened, Grace Kelly was in New York, promoting a picture in which she starred. She had a busy schedule but when I mentioned I wanted to discuss Gable she invited me to lunch.

"Have you spoken to him?" she asked.

"No, but I intend to."

"He's wonderful." I thought I detected a sigh over the phone. She was easy to talk to. She gave herself no airs.

"Yes," she smiled, "I found myself falling in love. Every woman does. He was what young girls dream about. He was older, but you forgot that when he looked at you. You realized only that you were a woman, and he was a man. Yet there was a small boy charm that made you want to mother him. There was nothing macho, just a gentleness and strength that came through in everything he did. You felt he could do anything, climb the highest mountain, knock out the heavy-weight champion with one punch, or run a blockade."

She laughed, thinking of an African incident. A little thing, but it told her a lot. At Christmas, Frank Sinatra had come on location to be with his wife, Ava.

The four decided to celebrate together. Ava, Frank, Grace and the King. They went to the one available restaurant. "There were some men at the bar. They had obviously been drinking for some time. They kept staring at our table. And making remarks. One of them finally staggered over to the table, whipped off his jacket, and challenged Sinatra to a fight. Sinatra had been fuming. He stood up and was about to go at it when the bartender threw the drunk out."

The next evening the scenario was replayed. This time the King was challenged. A different adversary, bigger and uglier, stood over him, breathing down his neck. "I can whip you," he cried. "You ain't so tough."

As the drunk struck a fighting stance, the King stood up and put his arm around him. They were about the same size. "Of course, you can," he said. "Now let me buy you a drink and wish you a Merry Christmas."

"It was amusing," Grace said, "seeing the difference between the two, Frank needing to prove himself, Clark so sure of himself he could afford to be generous."

I thought of the long African nights on location.

"Did you find him different?"

She smiled.

"He was everything you saw on the screen."

He was also a man's man. In one of his pictures he tore off his undershirt and tossed it aside, baring his chest. This created a crisis in the underwear market as men all over the world stopped wearing undershirts. He hunted and trapped, skied, flew a plane, wrangled horses. Yet he was known to walk old ladies across the street and dandle small children on his knee. He had little schooling, yet he read a book a day. His marvelous physique was no accident. At 15, he worked in the oil fields with his roustabout father, swinging a sledgehammer all day to develop the body that was the envy of athletes.

He often favored women not only plain but older than himself. But his great love was a blonde beauty, a wife who died when her plane crashed against the side of a mountain. He was shattered. For a while life meant little to him. Though over age, at 42, he went into the war a fighting private, and came out a fighting major, a bombardier, always the first to volunteer.

I had dug up enough on him for a book. I was ready to sit down with him. He was seeing everybody, they told me at 20th Century-Fox. Not like the old days at MGM where they kept the press from him and Garbo to enhance their mystiques.

Flying out to Hollywood, I picked up a magazine which bannered a story about Gable on its cover. It was one of those scandal magazines which attacked every virtue and magnified every frailty of a celebrity. He was pictured as an opportunist who had married two older women to improve his career and social standing. The writer described him as an inept lover. How he knew this I never knew. I read the article with a sinking feeling. It not only slandered a man I had grown to admire in studying him, but would, I knew, make our own meeting difficult.

My hunch was correct. Studio executives at Fox, responsible for setting up the interview, were embarrassed. Clark's agents had ruled out all meetings with the press. Clark was climbing back into the shell, which he had left briefly on joining a new studio.

The studio would have liked the story. He was a new star for them. Making a new movie, *Soldier of Fortune*. They wanted to launch him with a hail of publicity, and offset the scurrilous article. I needed the insight into Gable only he could give me.

Harry Brand, the studio executive in charge, gave me an appraising look. "There's one chance," he said.

Three younger aides laughed.

"Not a chance," they said.

Brand's eyes were fixed on me.

"I'm not telling you what kind of story to write. I'm only asking you. Will it be something he won't want to read?"

I smiled at his adroitness.

"All I can tell you is that I admire him."

He stood up and gave me a quizzical look.

"How many people do you admire?"

"Not very many. Not in my business."

He was gone no more than 10 minutes. He was smiling when he came back.

"Can you have lunch with Clark?"

There was an incredulous chorus from his aides.

"Harry, how did you do it?"

He waved an airy hand to show how simple it was.

"All I said was, 'Clark, I've known you for 30 years. If there's a gentleman in Hollywood it has to be you. This young fellow came 3,000 miles to talk to you. We told him to come. We didn't think there'd be any trouble.'"

Clark had been standing in the rear of a studio theater, watching rushes of the picture he was filming. Harry had never asked anything of him before.

He laughed and shook Harry's hand.

"Harry, you always knew how to get to me. Of course, I'll see him."

The first thing that struck me was his erect bearing. No West Point cadet stood straighter. He was almost 60. He turned to me with a smile. There was nothing guarded in his greeting. I saw the flash of his dark eyes and the dimples that endeared him to millions. His handshake was firm and dry. Seeing him up close was like seeing one of his movies. The husky voice, the gestures, the raised eyebrow. His body was trim and muscular, without an ounce of fat, his arms brawny and his hands like knotted steel. His hair was gray at the temples. His face weathered by sun and wind. He looked like the man who ran a Civil War blockade and fought off the Indians at Fort Laramie.

The writer on his picture was a former New York newspaperman. He had worked on a rival paper before he became
a Hollywood millionaire. We made small talk about his newspaper days in the short walk to the studio commissary.

As we reached the building we could hear the clang of fire
trucks in the street outside the studio gates.

Clark turned to his writer.

"Do you miss your newspaper days?"

"Oh, yes," came the rejoinder. "It was fun."

"I'm sure," I smiled, "you could get your old job back."

Clark grinned. "I made a newspaper picture. All the real
reporters wanted to know how they could become screen-
writers."

I had been a reporter on the newspaper where some of the
filming took place.

"I understand you gave everybody a raise."

The famous grin expanded. "I was a hardboiled editor who
rolled up his sleeves and barked out orders. Do they do that
anymore?"

"Some of them do."

He was relaxed. That was a good sign. He normally didn't
take lunch. This was his first visit to the Fox commissary. I
could see why when we walked in. It was as wide open as a
Wyoming range. There was no place he could sit without
being gaped at.

The room was crowded with stars, character actors, directors. There was a buzz as we walked through. Some of the
ladies dropped their forks. We were ushered into an L-shaped
angle of the dining room. Where only a handful of studio chiefs
dined. As Clark sat down, all the movie stars and directors
stood up and applauded. It was a spontaneous tribute from his
peers. He stood up and bowed. There was a smile on his lips,
and a mist in his eye. He was not of granite and steel.

I knew that having lunch didn't necessarily mean he would give me the help I wanted. I thought I would appeal to his sporting instinct, and humor, readily apparent in this man who played himself. To get around his well-known reluctance to discuss personal matters.

The food had arrived and he was toying with a salad. He didn't appear to be hungry. I braced myself and dove in.

"How about this?" I said. "I know there are things you don't normally talk about—personal things. Suppose I make a statement based on my research that I believe to be true. If true, all you have to do is nod. Then it will be me saying it, not you. If it isn't true, I'll throw it out."

He was amused.

"It sounds interesting."

My first statement had to be on the nose. Otherwise, it could be my last statement. And the game would be up.

I singled out something I was reasonably sure of, not of an intimate nature. Early on he had won an Oscar, filmdom's top award, for best actor in a delightful little comedy, *It Happened One Night*. The trophy had gathered dust in his study. One day the small son of a director friend picked it up and looked at it in admiration.

"If you like it," said Clark, "you can have it."

The boy's father protested. But Clark waved him down: "Let the youngster enjoy it."

Knowing anything about Clark, only one explanation offered itself. A blind man would have seen it.

"You gave your Oscar to that boy because it no longer meant anything to you when you didn't get the Oscar for your unforgettable performance as Rhett Butler in the greatest of all pictures."

He nodded and smiled, waiting for me to go on. There was an amused glint in his eyes. He was enjoying the game. My former colleague seemed entertained.

I turned to something else of interest and not abrasively sensitive. Something obvious from his rugged he-man nature.

"When you marry," I said, "you will marry a younger woman because you want a son you can teach to hunt and fish and be a man."

His smile widened. He was beginning to enjoy our little game, but it hadn't reached into any corridor of his life that was painful. I hesitated over my next question, as it went into the most tragic moment of his life. Yet it was crucial for it did turn his life around, making him dig deep within himself to find the God who would guide him through this heart-wrenching ordeal—the death of the woman he loved above all others, his wife, the brilliant, beautiful Carole Lombard. The actress whose life had blended with his until they were one. She had perished in a wartime bond-selling mission when her plane crashed on a mountainside near Las Vegas. Clark, stricken, was called on by authorities to climb the mountain and identify what was left of her remains in the charred wreckage of the plane. He sat in a daze, unable to move off the base at the foot of the mountain. He finally staggered to his feet to begin the mournful ascent. Eddie Mannix, the studio chief at MGM, stopped him.

"You shall remember her as she was. That's what she would want."

Clark shook himself and pushed ahead, so distraught he didn't realize what he was doing. Mannix held up an authoritative hand.

"I'm going," he told the shaken actor. "This is your boss talking. This is an order."

Clark nodded. It was important that he remember her as she looked when she laughed and smiled, and danced in his arms. For that was all he had now. A memory.

The other man, much older than Clark, climbed the mountain for his friend.

Years later when Mannix was dismissed, Clark left the studio.

I could see him waiting as all this turned over in my mind.

"You left the studio where you had been so many years when Eddie Mannix was fired. He climbed the mountain for you, you never forgot."

I saw a tear in his eye and moved on.

After Carole's death he was the target of many women. None more astute than a titled English lady who was actress enough to imitate the wit and humor of the wife he missed so much. I had noticed from pictures that she wore her hair and dressed like the wife he mourned. She talked like her, walked like her, laughed like her. Her name was Lady Ashley. She played the part to perfection.

"You were finally drawn into marriage with a blonde beauty who played your lost wife so well that you thought she was like her. Disenchanted when she became herself after the marriage, you ended the relationship. You realized you had been duped."

He put aside his salad, and gave me a surprised look.

"If you saw it," he said, "why didn't I?"

Any barriers between us were removed.

"Ask what you like," he said. "I may as well tell you about myself as have you tell me."

And so I asked him about his father, and to elaborate on the son he had never had but always wanted.

He took the larger reality first.

"I don't see much of my dad," he grinned. "I built him a house on my ranch as far from my house as possible. I try to keep out of his way. He's an independent spirit. I love him. I don't want him to feel dependent."

He missed not having a son, a boy he could hunt and trap and fish with, and watch grow up strong and straight.

He was reported to be courting Kay Spreckels, an attractive blonde socialite of childbearing age.

"I'm not ready for any announcements. The lady in question has something to say about that."

And if he married and it was a daughter?

He laughed. "It doesn't make that much difference nowadays. Girls ride and golf and go to sporting events, just like the boys."

I had a question from a goatish editor, which he had written out so there would be no mistake.

"Why do you think women all over the world fall in love with you?"

He didn't duck the question. He had been mobbed in public too often not to know how he was regarded. He had thought about it.

"I don't know that it's all that universal. I think many of them see something in me that's lacking in their lives. Of course there's no reality to it." He smiled. "They don't have to sit across the table from me when I burp or hold my head when it aches."

He asked if I would like to go through the rooms and memorabilia of his dead wife, saying he had never done this before. He had kept them just as they were at the time she was killed. I had no wish to pry. Besides I had my story.

The King Lives. Long Live the King.

My series ran in a number of papers across the country. I was out of the office the day the first article ran. He had read it back in California, and was not too busy to send me a wire. It was typical of his humor and his generosity.

"Congratulations. Did everything I could to promote your story. Married Kay today. Will be gone two weeks. Come out and visit us when we get back."

I would have liked nothing better. But in my absence my editor had run Clark's open wire with the story. On a front page. I was too young and embarrassed by this lack of taste to respond. Thinking he would consider the breach of taste mine.

He did have a son. He never saw him. He was born after Clark's death. It was one of the few prizes that eluded him.

I think of him often. He was the kind of a man I would like to have been. He had an interest in people. He asked about myself, my career, what aspirations I had. I don't remember any other celebrity having done this. I like to think of him as he really was. The Southern blockade runner, scoffing at the young hotbloods of the Deep South who thought they'd run the Yankees off in a couple of weeks. Standing there, with his hands on his hips, that mocking smile on his lips, telling them they were a bunch of spoiled brats, and stuffing it down their throats.

I know why he didn't get the Oscar he deserved. He made it look too easy. "Gable's not acting," they said. "He's only playing himself."

I had a continuing interest in Clark Gable and the Oscar he shunned. With his marriage to Kay Spreckels, the Oscar was returned to Clark's ranch home. Kay liked looking at it. Shortly after my Gable series ran in some 50 newspapers, the Motion Picture Academy, which had denied Clark an Oscar for his role in *Gone with the Wind*, put in a bid for the Oscar he won for the light comedy *It Happened One Night*. They thought the gold-plated statuette, no more than a foot high and more brass than gold, would make a nice museum piece.

Clark cheerfully gave the Academy first rights to buy the Oscar that had meant so little to him. Once it went on sale, he put a price of $10 on it—for the Academy—extending his feeling of its value in his eyes.

The marriage with Kay prospered. She was young enough to bear him the child he wanted. She was carrying that child when Clark, on desert location for the movie *Misfits*, suffered a fatal heart attack. Kay blamed his costar Marilyn Monroe, saying that her temperamental absences from the set had so exasperated Clark that he had been driven to wrangling the wild horses in the film to work off his frustration. Heavy duty for a man in his 60s. No longer the lusty star of *Gone with the Wind* or the rugged reporter of *It Happened One Night*.

Kay and Clark enjoyed a relationship that assuaged his grief over Carole Lombard's tragic death. A bereft Kay lived on bringing up the son, John, that Clark had longed for. Her love for Clark was undying until her own death. I remembered her telling me with a dewy eye, at a small gathering, that "Clark would be 80 years old today." This almost 20 years after his death.

The Oscar had been gathering dust all those years. The son put it on auction with other memorabilia of his father's some time after his mother's death. Christie's, the famous auction house, handled the sale which was the talk of Tinsel Town.

The Oscar, disdained by Clark, brought more than $600,000. Considerably more than Clark had been paid for many of his pictures. The Academy challenged the sale, claiming first rights. The judge ruled they had waited too long to notify John Gable and Christie's of their position. Clark would have smiled.

The buyer had been anonymous. But not for long, when it turned out he had given the Oscar to the Academy. The donor was a fan of Gable's, the enormously successful director Steven Spielberg. The Academy had persuaded him to make a statement. He said that he acted to keep "the only Oscar Clark Gable had received" from being exploited, finding a sanctuary in the Academy's museum.

"The only Oscar" . . . rooted in the mind of the very special director of *Schindler's List* and *Jurassic Park*. Thinking, like myself, of the Oscar denied Clark by the Academy for a very special role in a very special picture that would live as long as there were movies and people went to see them.

Actors

I was raving about what a wonderful guy Gable was. Warm, democratic, a great sense of humor, always courteous to the swarm of satellites who orbited around his star. The wardrobe woman got the deference of a queen, the makeup artist a bow, the lowliest extra a smile.

"The perfect professional," I said, "always on time, always prepared, never a sign of temper or temperament."

Nat Dychess, a publicity executive at the Fox studio, nodded thoughtfully. "Yes," he said, "he's the best. If there's a gentleman on the lot it's got to be Clark."

I noticed the slightest hesitation.

"You know," he went on, "I've been out here for 30 years, and there's nobody like him. I should know. I married an actress."

"He could have been anything," I enthused. "A successful politician, a general, an industrial giant, whatever he wanted to be."

"Yes," he said with a glimmer of a smile. "All you say is true. But you forget one thing."

I gave him a curious glance as we drove through the heart of Hollywood.

"And what is that?"

"He's an actor. "And," he paused, "actors aren't people."

I drew back in surprise.

"They are creatures apart. Creatures of fancy and ego. Figments of their imagination. A combination of reality and unreality. You're Rhett Butler and you're Clark Gable." He smiled. "You play Napoleon a while, you get to think you're Napoleon. If you're a good enough actor."

It was my turn to smile.

"And your wife, the actress?"

He smiled. "She plays Josephine."

Sir Michael

I loved Sir Michael Redgrave in *Thunder Rock*, a film about one man's heroic struggle against the pitiless sea. Sir Michael was now starring in the Broadway play, *Tiger at the Gates*, and I was delighted at the prospect of meeting my boyhood idol.

The play hadn't been doing well. I supposed the producers were looking for something that would stir some interest in a drama about the Trojan war. The hero was not any of the recognizable Greek heroes like Ulysses and Achilles. But Hector, the Trojan prince whose brother Paris had abducted the fair Helen. I could see where Hector, even if you spelled it right, would be a tough sell on Broadway.

I had checked Sir Michael out. English. Cambridge. Aloof. Didn't like Hollywood. Movies: Academy nomination for best actor, *Mourning Becomes Electra*; *The Lady Vanishes*; *The Quiet American*; *Dead of Night*; *Nicholas and Alexandra*. Two actress daughters, Lynn and Vanessa Redgrave, the only sisters to vie against each other for best actress award. A talented family.

Sir Michael was waiting in his dressing room. He didn't look much different from what he looked in *Thunder Rock*. The same craggy face and distant eye, the lean long body and the sculptured hands. He didn't rise to greet me, but indicated a chair with a wave of his hand. He sat waiting, his hands folded. I was about to say how much I had enjoyed his movie, but I saw he was in no mood for small talk. I sensed a gulf between us that had little to do with me, but more with my vocation. In his native England, at this time, two-penny journalists were treated like tradespeople and directed to the rear door.

I was groping about, conscious of his cold, unblinking stare. Then recalled, luckily, I thought, the bit about actors never getting to be themselves, but a multitude of people.

"It must be frustrating," I said, "to be always somebody other than yourself. Hector in ancient Troy, when you're Michael Redgrave, a knight of the British empire."

I saw an expression of immediate distaste.

"How about yourself?" he said with a voice that would have chilled an Eskimo. "You reporters are always feeding off somebody else, like a bunch of parasites."

I wasn't exactly floored. Reporters weren't all that popular. Except I hadn't expected anything like this from my hero.

"That may be true," I said. "But we're always ourselves. Parasitic journalists to you, hungry wolves to others. But we know what we are. The provenders of news, good or bad. We're always the same."

He sat unmoved, silent, not deigning a reply. I rose to my feet. There were no goodbyes or pleased-to-meet yous. He was no hypocrite.

I never did get to see the play. One tiger at the gate was enough. I catch *Thunder Rock* on television every once in a while. It was a great movie. He was a great actor. I had a feeling, though, that he wasn't always acting, not like some actors. In his dressing room that day, I had an idea his was a role rather unique even for him. He was playing himself.

Vanderbilt

*A*lfred Vanderbilt was known for improving the breed. He was president of Belmont racetrack in New York and Pimlico in Maryland. He bred his thoroughbreds in Kentucky and his three-year-old Native Dancer would have won all his races had he not stumbled coming out of the gate in the Kentucky Derby.

Going to the racetrack with Alfred was like going to bat with Babe Ruth. It was an occasion. He had a horse running at Belmont, and I was doing a story.

"You might talk to my trainer, Bill Winfrey," he said, "and get the feel of the track."

He gave me a fill-in on his horse. His name was Find. He had been racing in California with mixed results. He was of a good blood line, and Alfred liked him like he liked every horse in his stable. He was the same way with people. He didn't care if a man was a Rockefeller or a Vanderbilt, or a reporter.

We proceeded to Alfred's box. I soon saw he was the cynosure of all eyes. There must have been 20,000 people in the stands wondering who Alfred liked in the fifth.

He suggested we visit the stables where I could talk to his trainer, the same who had trained the immortal Native Dancer. The jockey, Eric Guerin, was already astride the horse. Winfrey and Guerin were talking together. "The distance is right," Winfrey was saying. "And the horse is right. Let him run his race. It should be a walk-in."

Guerin nodded. And then took off on a leisurely ride to the paddock, where the horses would be reviewed by students of the breed.

As we started back to his box I could see Alfred eyeing me with amusement. I guess he knew what was on my mind.

"Are you making a bet?" I said as we settled back in his box.

"I never bet a race," he said. "It would immediately get around who I had bet on." He smiled. "I wouldn't want anyone to lose any money because of me. Anything can happen in a horse race. Otherwise the favorites would always win."

I remembered Native Dancer's bad start in the Derby and could readily agree.

He saw me consulting the *Racing Form* and going over the program.

"If you want to bet, just make it a small bet. And don't go straight to the betting window. Someone may follow you, thinking you have it from the horse's mouth."

I wasn't much of a handicapper. But I would have picked Find if I was sitting in the cheapest seat in the grandstand. He was a big horse. He looked strong, and the odds were right—five to one. I suppose I could have sat the race out. But who went to the track without making a bet? Only Vanderbilt.

I took a circuitous route to the betting windows, looking around as I left the box. I didn't see anybody following me, though an elderly man with a cane did stop to ask the way to the men's room. He could have been a spy, but I questioned it, since I followed him into the men's room to throw any snooper off the trail. He seemed to have only one concern. I then stole back into the betting area and waited just before the gong closed off the betting to place my bet. Twenty dollars.

I settled back in the box, tingling with excitement. I was looking for a stirring race, with my horse storming into the back stretch to take it by a nose. It didn't happen that way. Find won in a romp. It was the easiest hundred dollars I'd ever made.

Alfred didn't ask if I'd won or lost. He didn't have to. All he had to do was look at my face.

Winning had its problems. I wasn't sure whose money I had bet. Mine or the newspaper's. I solved it by taking my editor to dinner. I knew Alfred wouldn't mind. All he cared about was improving the breed.

Old Blue Eyes

I had not heard from the caller for a year. He was a tipster, who occasionally gave me a lead on a story. He always made a mystery of everything.

"There is somebody very important who would like to talk to you," he said in his stilted fashion.

I waited, knowing it had to be something to bring him out of retirement.

"This person would like to meet with you. He has a story to tell. He wants to tell it."

"Who is it?"

He mentioned a name. The world-famous crooner. Old Blue Eyes himself. Frank Sinatra.

"Why me? I've never met him."

"You got the biggest circulation. That's why. If you worked for the Podunk Herald, he wouldn't look at you."

We agreed on a time and place. I was to meet him that night at the club where he was performing, an hour or so before he was to go on.

"Bring a date," said the tipster. "He don't mind."

He never minded a pretty face. He had a bit of a Tough Guy reputation, but the ladies found him charming. It was remarkable how many young women were willing to break whatever engagements they had to dine with me that evening. And he was not good-looking, and had skinny legs.

The owner of the Manhattan club greeted us with a bow. "I'm to give you the best table, and the best of everything. He is delayed."

There was no question who *he* was. Still the King of the Swooners, though his television show had been canceled and Hollywood was no longer wooing. He was in one of his declines.

We had a drink in the lounge and waited. A frantic young man who I took to be his press agent hovered about.

"What is this all about?" he said. "What is Frank up to? Why is he meeting you?"

"I haven't the slightest. Why not ask him? He'll be here in a few minutes."

At this point there was a stir at the door, and he made his entrance, smiling, waving, signing an autograph or two for the swooners and shaking hands. He looked like you saw him in the movies or on the bandstand. He was electric. Even not singing in that sexy baritone, you could feel his presence. I looked at my date, a beautiful girl, fairly sophisticated, from a society family. Her lips were parted and her eyes were glowing. I had seen that look before, on the faces of women looking at Gable. It was a magnetism, a charisma, an extension of the individual, that exploded in public and on the screen, through some inexplicable combination of hormones and chromosomes.

He sat down with an appreciative look for the girl, and a firm handclasp for me that spoke of sincerity. As he spotted the press agent, the smile faded. He beckoned him with a finger. "Didn't I tell you I didn't want you here?" His face darkened and the Tough Guy emerged. "Beat it."

I saw my date blink in surprise. But soon he was all smiles. Mister Charm. And her eyes were aglow again.

I looked at my watch.

"We don't have much time."

He apologized. "It was a testimonial for an old friend. Joe DiMaggio. I couldn't help myself. I'll get to the point."

He didn't seem at all flustered, smooth and amiable, as he got into his story. It had something to do with a blind item in a Broadway gossip column. I couldn't understand why he would get steamed up since no names had been mentioned. It was one of those "What well-known singer and what well-known actress" things, where you had to guess who it was if you cared that much.

The singer and his wife, presumably Ava Gardner, had presumably quarreled in their plush hotel suite across the street from Central Park. Ava announced she was dashing out to meet an old flame whose band was making music nearby. He, the crooner, threatened to shoot himself if she walked out. She was in the hall when he fired three shots into the park, and she kept on going.

That was the scenario.

I shrugged, not seeing what he wanted of me.

"I want to repudiate the story once and for all. It's embarrassing."

"I don't see why it should bother you. It could be anybody."

"A lot of people read these columns and pick the names out. It's come back on me already."

His records had given me countless hours of pleasure. He was like a friend singing a love story to somebody I loved.

"You'll only give the rumors more attention," I said, wondering what my editor would think. He was news, even if his show had just been canceled.

He shook his head. "Rumors have a way of growing. They brought in the police."

My head went up. And my antenna.

He went into greater detail. He was settled in his suite on the 33rd floor of the Hampshire House, when there was a stir in the hall outside and a pounding on the door. It was the police. There was never any fondness between him and the police because of his tendency to consort with questionable characters. He barely opened the door.

"What's the problem?"

"We're answering a call about a shooting on the 33rd floor," an officer said.

He jerked his slim shoulders.

"Why bother me? There's a big producer and his actress wife staying down the hall. Maybe he shot her, or they shot each other."

They were looking for a gun, but they had no search warrant. He wouldn't let them in. But it was a scary experience. It got worse the next day when they followed a look-alike associate of his, Manny Sachs of NBC, up the hotel elevator and insisted on searching the place.

Sachs, intimidated, looked on helplessly as they rifled through the dresser drawers.

I had been listening closely.

"Did they find the gun?"

He gave me a pained look.

"How could they find what was never there?"

I was mystified. I couldn't see what he was getting at, or how I could be of help.

"I don't see what you have to be afraid of. They have nothing on you."

I could see that he expected me to jump at the story. He looked disappointed and defensive.

"My producer, Paul Dudley, can vouch for my story. I was sitting around chatting with him and his wife when the police came. Ask him about it."

As he told me the story, I was trying to figure out why he was telling it to me. He was a sophisticated man. He knew what the repercussions would be. His denying the stories would only give them new life. He had a well-known aversion for personal publicity, and this was not like him or his image.

"Why are you going to all this trouble? At most it's a guessing game. And it's anybody's guess."

He hesitated, and I thought I caught a glimmer of fear in the famous blue eyes.

"It's the police. They're trying to frame me. They would have put a gun in my apartment if my friend hadn't been there. I want them to know I'm not running scared."

I felt a vague uneasiness. There was something missing. Something I didn't know about. I didn't like knocking the police about without knowing more about it.

I wanted to talk to Ava and get her side of it. She wasn't available. She had left for Spain on a picture assignment— *The Barefoot Contessa*. That stopped me for a moment.

"If she wasn't in the apartment, where was she when the argument and the shooting supposedly took place?"

He was offhand about it. "Some kind of a shower, something like that. You know how women are."

I could hardly imagine Ava Gardner at a baby shower.

Somehow it didn't add up. He was exposing himself to disagreeable publicity without anything to gain as I saw it.

"Anything you do is news. We'll be glad to print your side of it. But you'll be acquainting millions of people with a juicy bit of your private life they hadn't heard of before."

He studied me for a moment with a puzzled look.

"Why are you telling me this? I thought you'd jump at it."

"You may think twice about it, once the uproar starts. The police won't take the accusations sitting down."

"Thanks, but I want to go ahead with it. I'll call you at noon tomorrow. We'll finish up."

He looked at his watch and started to rise.

I held up a hand. I had my misgivings. It was all too easy. "Just so there won't be any confusion, I'll type out the notes as we go along, and you can initial each page."

I didn't like tape recorders. They impeded the flow of a conversation. I had an idea he would talk more freely without one.

He nodded, smiling. He was in good spirits.

I gave him my home phone number. My pretty companion looked as if she would have liked to do as much with hers.

We shook hands.

"I'll call you," he repeated as he went off to perform.

The next day passed without a call, and the next. On the third day a copy boy bustled over to my desk with the afternoon newspapers. There was a smiling picture of the crooner at the airport. He was overseas bound. Spain, and *The Barefoot Contessa*.

Just another one of those columns. Everything was coming up roses for the crooner and his gal. Who ever heard of anybody firing a gun into the park from the 33rd floor of a hotel. What could they hit?

That evening I had dinner with a former actor, John Conte, at a Manhattan restaurant patronized by the theatrical fraternity. We had just settled ourselves when a youngish man with a wild eye and a drink in his hand, wandered over to say hello. I didn't catch his name. As he picked his way back to the bar, I asked Conte:

"What does that man do?"

He registered surprise.

"That's Paul Dudley, Sinatra's producer. His show was just canceled. I guess he's drowning his sorrow."

There were butterflies in my stomach. This was the man Sinatra had wanted me to talk to. The man he had been with the night the police dropped in to investigate the firing of three bullets into the park. I glanced over at the bar. Dudley was sitting alone. He looked somewhat the worse for wear. He had one elbow on the bar, and had motioned for another drink. He looked like he had the limit.

I looked at Conte.

"Mind if I talk to him for a few moments?"

He shrugged. "Don't expect too much. He's drinking."

Dudley was cordial. Drinking has that effect on some people.

He called over to the bartender.

"Give the man a drink."

He gave me the all-knowing smile of a man who had too much to drink and can handle it.

"Too bad about your show," I said, introducing myself, in case he hadn't caught my name at the table.

He gulped down his drink. "Nothing's going right. Lady Luck kicked our butt."

I mentioned that Sinatra had appeared to be in good spirits.

"Yeah, he bounces well. He'll come back. He always comes back. That's Old Blue Eyes for you."

"We had a date and he broke it."

He ordered another drink.

"Yeah, I know about that."

He looked a little woozy. At the rate he was bending his elbow I knew I would have to talk fast.

"Have you any idea why he didn't keep the date?"

He looked at me in surprise.

"You mean you don't know?"

I shook my head. "I understand you were there the night things supposedly happened. The star witness."

He looked solemn and all-wise, like an owl.

"You bet I am. I was sitting there with Old Blue Eyes when the cops came pounding on the door. Just like gang-busters. He stood up to them. They didn't like it. They said they'd be back."

"I don't see why he broke our date. He was so emphatic about getting all this on the record."

He pushed down another drink. He was too tipsy to guard his tongue, yet sober enough to know what he was saying.

"So you want to know why he didn't meet you?"

He leered, almost slipping off his barstool.

"I'll tell you why," he said, preening himself. "I told him not to. That's why."

I looked at him in amazement.

"You told him? Why would you do that?"

He laughed so hard he almost fell over backwards.

"Because the story was true. Every last word of it. He knew who Ava was going out to meet. Artie Shaw, her ex-husband, playing with his small musical group on Broadway. And he yelled, 'If you walk out of this room, I'll kill myself.' So when she walked out, slamming the door, he picked up the gun and fired across the street into the park. He figured he wouldn't hit anything but a squirrel. You could hear the shots a block away. She didn't come back. She kept right on going."

The thought seemed to amuse him. But for only a moment.

His head had sunk almost to the bar. He was mumbling. "He wanted to get the police off his tail. Put them on the defensive." His eyes were closed now, and his voice fuzzy. "He told me about meeting with a reporter and I told him, 'Forget it. Don't mess with the police. You're asking for trouble.'"

I thanked him for the drink. He didn't hear me. He had bombed out on the bar.

Elvis
(The Beginning)

"**I**'d like you to meet our new star," the studio executive said. "A 21-year-old kid from Mississippi." He smiled. "He's got the charisma of Valentino and sings better than Sinatra."

Elvis Presley had just finished a scene from his first picture, *Love Me Tender*, and was mopping his brow in the hot sun.

He was friendly, but resigned to the usual bag of questions about how it felt to be a Hollywood star, and the rage of so many young women who melted at his look.

I could see he was bored, until the studio man mentioned I was from *The New York Daily News*.

"You're from *The News*?" His eyes snapped. "You're just the man I want to talk to." He wasn't angry, but there was a certain fire in his eyes, and his Southern drawl was a little heavier than it had been.

"Do you know that Mister Gross," he went on. "The television writer on that paper?"

I nodded. I knew Ben Gross very well. He was not only a colleague but a neighbor. A small, elderly man, with a scholarly background. He had an absentminded way of walking down the street with a bundle of newspapers, reading along as he walked, bumping into people and sometimes a lamppost. He was a gentle man and wouldn't hurt a fly.

"Yes," I said, "I know him. He's a fine writer and a gentleman."

"Well," he said, "that man done took me down the river."

I hadn't heard the expression before. I gathered the river was the Mississippi, and the trip a figure of speech.

"What did Mister Gross write about you?"

He sputtered a moment in his indignation. "He wrote I was a bad influence on teenagers because of the way I moved my body when I sang." His voice rose and I could see the pained look. He was greatly distressed. "Mister Gross called me Elvis the Pelvis. That really hurt. I'm not like that."

He reached out and took my hand with this burst of emotion. "I'd appreciate your talking to Mister Gross, tell him I'm not that kind of person. I don't want to hurt anybody. Please tell Mister Gross that for me."

I could see the studio man was puzzled. I didn't know what to make of it. I realized I was listening to an unusual young man who cared about people and wanted people to care about him. I found his respect for his elders touching.

I shook his hand. "I'll certainly be glad to let him know how you feel."

He thanked me up and down. "I'd be very grateful to you, sir."

A couple of days later I ran into Ben Gross on the street in New York where we lived. He had the usual pile of papers under his arm, and was trudging home after a day of watching television and writing about it.

I mentioned my meeting with Elvis. And what he had asked of me.

Ben's gray face brightened and a smile came to his lips. "I

didn't know anybody under 30 read my column," he said. "He's a very nice young man even if he does move his hips in a way he shouldn't."

Elvis
(The Legend Begins)

blue light flashed over Elvis' humble home the night he was born. It streaked across the Southern sky like a comet. Vernon Presley, standing outside in the crisp January air, wondered for a moment whether this son he would name Elvis Aaron Presley would have a life as exalted as the light he saw.

He was a different kind of performer. And a different kind of human being. He not only loved everybody. He didn't know what it was not to love. When he was six years old in his Tupelo, Mississippi, birthplace, he saw a neighbor boy smile wistfully as he pedaled by on the tricycle his share-cropper parents had saved and scrimped for. Elvis got off the tricycle and gave it to the boy. "It's yours," he said. "You ride it."

His parents reclaimed the tricycle. Elvis gave it back to the boy. The parents looked at each other and shrugged. And Vernon Presley wondered again about the blue light that had flashed over his house that night. Had this son been born in this humble home to speak to the world of love? A love that spoke in many tongues.

As an adult he gave an expensive piece of jewelry to his friend and fellow performer, Sammy Davis Jr.

A friend said, "Why did you do that? Sammy is a very wealthy man."

Elvis smiled. "Rich people need to know they're loved, too."

He was always seeking, wondering at the pact between him and the Lord. And the blue light. Would he ever grasp its meaning? He was handsome, rich, world-famous. Women swooned over him, men envied him. And yet he felt empty. He knew there was more. There had to be more. Going from one cookie-cutter movie to another, singing rock, rock, rock-around-the-clock, mobbed by crowds clutching at his clothes for some memento of his fame and charisma.

One day he was introduced to the spiritual by a young man who had called to trim his hair. They talked together for hours. And stayed together for years. Elvis learned to know about Jesus the man, and what he stood for, the miracles he performed, the people he embraced with his love. He learned about the Jews of old, and the mighty prophets, of Moses and Elijah, and Isaiah, who had prophesied the coming of Christ, the Son of Man, who would show life was everlasting.

He learned about the Yogis, the teachers of ancient India, who blandly accepted other faiths, Christianity, Judaism, Buddhism, and worshiped at their shrines as though they were their own.

He was a frequent visitor to the Self-Realization Center in Los Angeles, founded by the Hindu teacher, Yogananda, whose teachings seemed little different from Christ's.

"Overcome evil by good, sorrow by joy, cruelty by kindness, ignorance by wisdom. And spread a spirit of brotherhood among all peoples."

He felt elevated by his conversations with the teachers at the Yogananda monastic center atop Mount Washington in

Los Angeles. All appeared tranquil and at peace, in refreshing contrast to the noise and turmoil of the street and marketplace.

Between his musical chores he studied with the monks in their mountain retreat and at their lake shrine in Pacific Palisades. Study, he found, was not enough. He had to experience peace and tranquility deep within himself through meditation, to free himself of vexatious distractions. He would frequently call on the head of the Self-Realization Center, Sri Daya Mata, the former Fay Wright, an American. He thought of her as his spiritual mother. When his marriage with Priscilla, his twin spirit, ended, he was shattered in mind and body. His hands trembled and he sat quietly in pain, his eyes closed to hide the tears.

Daya Mata understood. She knew he was feeling the burden of guilt the sensitive invariably suffer. For his heart had left Priscilla long before she left him. "We learn more from suffering," said Daya Mata, "but with every ending there is a new beginning."

The tranquility of the Yogis had captivated him. He thought he would make a new beginning in the monastery. "I would like to be one of you and work with people as you do, helping them as you have helped me."

She smiled. "You belong to the world, Elvis. God gave you that voice and made you what you are so you can trumpet his message to a world larger than ours."

He looked at her, not comprehending for a moment.

"Sing the songs that tell of your love for the Lord. Songs that will bring the millions into your fold. You will be a shepherd of the Lord."

And so came his recording of the unforgettable "How Great Thou Art." He felt inspired, fulfilled, as though he was, in truth, a channel of the Lord.

Despairing people everywhere, listening, took heart and prayed to the God who they felt had abandoned them. Elvis was exalted, exhilarated, freed of his world-weariness. Enjoying a new love affair with the millions who loved him.

His new faith removed many fears from his life. The fear of flying, the fear of living, the fear of dying. A youthful fear of being alone had begun to abate. Not by chance did he choose *Where No One Stands Alone* as the title for his gospel album. He had come to believe the Kingdom of the Lord was inside him.

Once he no longer feared death he thought about it in realistic terms. Death fascinated him. He saw it as a new beginning. Only a few days before he collapsed in his Memphis home, he predicted his imminent death to a young cousin, who was appalled. Elvis only smiled. "I have an idea," he said, "that I may be meeting an old friend." He touched the cross he invariably wore.

There was no doubt who he meant. The great figure for whom a light had also appeared in the sky. In whose birth sign of Capricorn he had been born. He had done all he could do. His spiritual songs would live as long as there were singers to sing them and people to listen. He had captured the heart of a people, generations behind and others yet to come.

His time had come. He had no regrets. His body had become heavy with the pain-killers he took to palliate the cancer that had invaded his bones. Only a tiny circle of friends knew of the pain he lived with day and night. In the mortuary, as he lay naked on a table, all the excess weight appeared to have left him. He looked lean and hard, as he had in his youth. Larry, the young yoga teacher who loved him, trimmed his hair, and Charlie Hodge, a beloved companion, touched up his face. They remembered Elvis looking at his swollen hands and saying, "I'll look like my old self one day."

Charlie's eyes misted as he rolled his mind back over the years. They had been like brothers. He bent down and kissed Elvis' cheek.

"When the Lord calls you home," he said softly, "you can't be late."

Tracy and Hepburn

They were throwing a big bash for the world premiere of *Edison the Man* in West Orange, New Jersey, home of Thomas Edison, the great inventor who had invented the electric light bulb, the phonograph and motion pictures while nodding himself to sleep. There were a host of dignitaries: the late inventor's son, Governor Charles Edison, a former Secretary of the Navy; a number of Hollywood celebrities and a flock of industrial giants. But the magnet was the star, playing the title role. The redoubtable, mercurial Spencer Tracy. Celebrated not only for his talent on the silver screen but his explosive temper.

He was very much in the news. Though married, his name had been romantically linked with his costar in many pictures, the beautiful and glamorous Katharine Hepburn—conspicuously absent at the much publicized event.

Jake, our city editor, was excited.

"This is the biggest social event in the history of New Jersey," he sputtered between his broken teeth. "Get to Tracy, see what's going on with him and Hepburn."

I was young and idealistic. "The man's married," I said.

"Married, schmarried," he came back with his usual wit.

"How about the movie and dinner?" "That's covered."

He looked at me. "Ever see any Tracy-Hepburn movies? They're electric."

"Like Edison?"

He glared as only Jake could glare. With eyes like flaming coals.

"Don't be a smart ass."

I'd seen *Dr. Jekyll and Mr. Hyde*, *Captains Courageous*, *Men of Boys Town*. All Tracy. But no Hepburn. "What do I ask him?"

His eyebrows went up a mile. "What do you ask him? You don't ask." He waved a couple of fingers in my direction. "You say you heard he's living with the woman. And they might be getting married."

"And so where did I hear it?"

"You just now heard it. Clean out your ears."

I'd been working for Jake for several months now. And like the other young reporters couldn't figure out what his problem was. He made everything look so simple. When it wasn't. Maybe it was because he never worked the street like we did.

"All right," I said. "Do I call it in?"

"You bring it in, and write it. We'll overnight it."

I heard him screaming as I got to the door. "And don't come back without something."

The party was in progress when I arrived. Cocktails were floating around the big room. Everyone was talking at once. The noise was deafening. The dinner and movie hadn't happened yet. I spotted Tracy right away. He was standing off, like he would like to be somewhere else. Anyplace else. Every once in a while somebody would brace him for an autograph. Usually a woman—a younger woman. Women liked him. He looked like a man who could handle himself. Women liked that.

A heavyset man with some presence was standing next to him. They appeared to be offhand with each other. I caught the man's eye, and he smiled. His name was John Considine. He was the producer. I guessed he smiled a lot when they launched a picture. Especially when it had his name on it.

I tried to appear casual. Friendly, yet business-like. I caught Tracy's eye. "I'm a reporter," I said, "for a Newark newspaper. We cover the county and most of the state."

He didn't say anything. He looked at me like he'd just tasted something rank. Considine's smile faded. His face had become like a sphinx. Immobile.

"Yes?" he said.

I nodded at Tracy. I decided to use the collective we. That seemed to make it less personal. To me anyway.

"We were just wondering about Mr. Tracy and Miss Hepburn."

The actor's body appeared to tense. His jaw set and his eyes were hard. I saw Considine edge closer to him out of a corner of my eye. We were about three or four feet apart. Tracy's eyes were like agates now. He finally spoke, in a voice like a whipsaw going through redwood.

"What do you want to know?" I paused a moment. Meanwhile thinking this was hardly the kind of thing I thought I'd be doing when I dreamed of being a reporter. Yet I knew names were news. And these were two of the biggest names in the world. Wherever movies were shown.

I finally got it out. There was no easy way of saying it. I heard each word as it rattled out of my mouth. "We understand that you and Miss Hepburn are living together and may soon get married."

It all happened so quickly. Tracy, cursing, lunged at me with his fist upraised. And Considine, moving swiftly, threw his arms around Tracy.

A dozen thoughts raced through my mind. Should I throw up my arms, waiting for a punch, sidestep or lash back? We were about the same size. I, 25 years younger. I'd been moved on before. You couldn't be a reporter and not get in some sort of scrape, like being thrown down stairs by a bunch of striking stevedores who didn't like your publisher's editorials.

Considine, with some effort, had taken a grip on Tracy, who stood fuming, still looking like he'd have a go at it.

"Spence," Considine was saying. "You'll just blow it up."

And then he turned to me. "You better move along."

I cabbed back to the paper, feeling like an idiot. It had never occurred to me to reject the assignment, or slough it off. But it was the last time I worked on any story I was that uncomfortable with.

I didn't know what to do about Jake. In his domain he could do no wrong. He was so worked up he jumped up when I trudged into the City Room.

"What happened?" he cried.

I told him. Not leaving anything out. "I have no story."

His lips twisted in a scornful smile. "No story. What do you mean no story? If the guy had taken a poke at you, we'd be on every front page." He wagged his head in disgust. "I had it all laid out. Like a movie. And you loused it up. You didn't get him mad enough."

The Lion

*E*verybody loved Paddy Doyle. He was a little man with a whimsical humor who loved to spin stories about his old friend, the immortal Irish singer, John McCormack. As far as we could gather they had gone to school together in Paddy's native Ireland, where Paddy had pointed himself toward the priesthood until with a mind bent of his own he became a journalist and came to this country.

He had only one fault as a journalist, a failing he shared with a good many others in a profession of brilliant but sometimes fragile souls. Every now and then, when the travails of an uncertain world were a little too much, he would take a wee bit of the Irish, and perhaps a bit more, and disappear for two or three days. Returning to his reporter's desk fresh-faced, though a little bleary-eyed, with new zest and a new story about his old friend, the immortal John.

He would have been long gone had it not been for peer pressure, and a managing editor who loved to listen to his stories, as the rest of us did. Except for terrible-tempered Jake, the city editor who didn't like the idea of sending a reporter out on a story and not getting a story back for maybe 48 hours.

"Let him be, Jake," said the managing editor with a twinkle in his eye. "One day when the immortal McCormack goes off to greener fields, Paddy will reward us with a story of McCormack's life that will bring tears of joy to our many Irish readers."

Jake would grit his false teeth, and think of some assignment that would keep his *bête noire*, this mild-mannered soft-spoken man he thought of as his nemesis, within walking distance of the newspaper—*The New Jersey Star-Ledger*.

One day, as we all listened, he summoned a penitent Paddy to the city desk with an imperious wave of his hand and a bark. "Doyle."

Paddy jumped up and approached Jake with a cautious step. For Jake was the only man on the editorial floor that called him anything but Paddy. As Paddy stood hat in hand at his desk, Jake snarled.

"I got an assignment for you, Doyle. At the Douglas Hotel, only two blocks away. An interview with a lion-tamer." He looked up at the big clock overhead. "It's 11 o'clock. I want you back in the office no later than two, three hours. Enough for any interview."

Paddy swallowed two or three times. "But my lunch, Jake?"

"You can drink that later." He picked up a copy of one of the New York papers that had been lying on his desk. "Have you read where your old friend, the Great Immortal, is mortally ill?"

Paddy nodded, and a tear came to his eye. "Yes, Jake," Paddy said in a gentle voice. "I lit a candle for him last night."

The managing editor happened to walk up to the city desk at this time. He put his arm around Paddy. "Maybe we should have Paddy put together something about his recollections of the great man. It would give us an intimate touch nobody else will have when . . ." He broke off with respect for Paddy's feelings.

This mark of affection seemed to touch off a chord of anger in the city editor. "He can do that later, when he gets back from the assignment."

He looked at Paddy and growled. "Now get going. I don't want any excuses."

Paddy sidled off in the curious way he had of taking shuffling steps.

The managing editor's eyes followed him. "You're hard on him, Jake. The man is suffering. He's losing more than a friend. The dream of a lifetime. Of happier days when they were both young."

Jake looked over at me. I had been standing at the desk, waiting for my assignment. He was in a worse humor than usual.

"What do you want?"

"You wanted to see me."

I didn't like Jake very much.

The managing editor walked off, shaking his head. I had heard him talk once of Jake's nose for news. I imagined that's why Jake was still around. He had a way of telling a young reporter like myself what to expect when he sent him out on a story, which made me ask him once why I couldn't just go back to my desk and write it like he said.

"Don't be a wise guy," he said. "Not around me."

He was looking at me now with a jaundiced eye. "Yeah, about that assignment. I want you hanging around until Doyle gets back."

That's all he said. I knew what he meant. I was glad to go back to my desk and work on a crossword puzzle if it meant helping Paddy.

I had finished the one puzzle, and was working on another, when Jake came over to my desk with a scowl and a look at the clock. He fumed. "You better get over to the Douglas, and find out what's keeping Doyle. We got an AP bulletin saying they don't expect McCormack to live out the day."

I got the lion-tamer's name and room number and started off when he said, "Now don't you get lost."

I forget what the lion-tamer's name was. But it sounded Hungarian-like, with a lot of Z's and Y's in it. Unpronounce-able. If you didn't know how it went.

I knocked on the door. A dark-haired man with a foreign look opened it tentatively. "Well?" he said through the narrow opening.

"I'm from the paper. Is Paddy Doyle here?"

"Oh, come in." He opened the door wide and shook my hand. He seemed almost relieved. He had a small suite. I looked around the living-room. No Paddy. I figured he might be in the bathroom.

The lion-tamer was about 40. About middle height, with a muscled chest and brawny arms. He looked uncomfortable.

"No, he left about an hour ago. I thought he might have gone back to the newspaper."

My nose for news, though not as long as Jake's, told me something must be wrong.

"Would you like to see the lion?" He gave me an ingratiat-ing smile.

I started. "You mean he's here?"

"Yeah, in the bedroom. I'll bring him out."

He caught my look. "He's harmless. Usually."

"Usually?"

He grinned apologetically.

"Well, Paddy went to pat him. And he nipped his hand. Just a little nip."

"The lion bit Paddy?"

"He'd never done it before. I think it was the smell of alco-hol. That bothers some lions. You haven't been drinking?"

I shook my head. Poor Paddy. That's all he needed. Bitten by a lion in a hotel room. I didn't have to ask how the interview had gone. It had gone with Paddy. Out the door. And his friend not expected to live out the day.

I felt as though my character was being tested. "Yeah, bring out the lion. Just keep him on leash."

He smiled. A little nervous, I thought. I wasn't that cool. He disappeared for a couple of minutes, making me wonder what was taking that long. He finally brought out the lion. He was big, bigger than the room. He was licking his chops; looking at me expectantly.

"I just fed him. Five pounds of fresh hamburger. A couple of swallows. You can pat him if you like."

"No thanks. I have to get going."

"What about the story? You know, we're appearing together on the stage. Paddy left so quickly I didn't get a chance to give him the time."

I took the time and weaseled my way out. The lion was still looking at me, with that same look. The lion-tamer grabbed my hand.

"Give my best to Paddy. I hope he got a good story."

It was a five-minute walk back to the paper. I envisioned Jake having a stroke. Though it did make a good little story when you thought about it. "Lion Bites Hand of Inquiring Reporter." Or, "Lion Makes News."

Jake looked up when I came in.

"So where's that inebriate?" he bellowed. "McCormack died. We just got the bulletin. Where the hell is Doyle?"

I shrugged. "I don't know. The lion bit him."

"The lion bit him? Are you on the stuff, too?"

"Honest, Jake. I saw the lion. If you want, I'll call the lion-tamer and have him bring the lion over. For pictures."

Jake glowered. "I told you. Stop being a wise guy."

"I just thought it would make a helluva story."

"Never mind that."

He yelled out three names and as many reporters responded on the run. He gave them a fierce look. "I want you guys to check every bar in the area. Bring in Doyle dead or alive. Dead or alive he's going to write that obit."

The managing editor had heard the commotion and stepped out of his office.

"I told you, Jake. You shouldn't have let him out of your sight." There was a mild reproof in his voice that gave Jake pause.

"All right," said Jake. "So we have a reporter you can't trust two blocks away."

I turned to the managing editor. "The lion bit Paddy."

The managing editor's eyebrows reached for the ceiling.

"The lion bit Paddy?"

I had never known him to laugh before. I thought he wouldn't stop. He finally subsided.

"He's all right?"

"Just a nip on the hand."

"And you saw the lion?"

"Oh, yes. He was licking his chops."

He took the matter out of Jake's hands. He looked at the three reporters standing around, trying hard not to smile. "Well, you men have listened to Paddy's stories about John McCormack for years. How about putting them together for a tribute to the great singer." He looked at Jake. "And we'll put Paddy's byline on it."

Paddy turned up three days later. Expecting to be fired. To pick up his last pay check. He had a bandage on his hand.

"I sure miss John," he said with a misty eye. "He was all I had."

The Millionaire

He looked very lean, self-assured, faintly condescending. He was not yet 30, and he was many times a millionaire. I looked at him across a huge desk. No papers, no little oddments, no telephone. Nothing distracting, except the nakedness of the glass-topped surface.

"How did you do it?" I said. "You must be very clever."

He spread his fingers against the top of the desk and smiled.

"Not at all. Just smart enough to hire people smarter than I am and don't know what to do with their smarts. I get them from the colleges. They're vastly underpaid. Psychologists, economists, marketing experts, internationalists. Authorities on human behavior. Why people do what they do and like what they like."

He spoke casually. A bit patronizing, I thought. Maybe because we were the same age and I felt I was doing very well at that time as a newspaper reporter, making some $300 a week.

"And how do you turn all this into millions of dollars?"

I tried keeping any negative feelings I had out of my voice.

"Very simple," he said. "My marketing expert researched the commodity markets, here and abroad. He gave me an advisory saying that silk would be in short supply for a few years because of world unrest. I passed this information on to my human behavior man. He advised me this would create a great demand for silk wear—particularly ladies' wear. Can you imagine a woman wearing nylons when silk stockings were available?"

"And so you got into the silk business?"

He smiled. "I *became* the silk business. I brought in my two geniuses on commodity trading and marketing. With their help I came as close as anyone could to cornering the silk market."

"May I ask how this was done?"

"All very legal. It didn't take as much money as you might think, the commodity market being what it is."

At that time I hadn't heard how some people ran a thousand dollars into a hundred thousand in commodity trading in a very short time. But I was ready to give him whatever he said. It had certainly worked for him.

"And this was all there was to it?"

He shook his head. "By no means. I brought in my psychologist and human behavior specialist. What they said decided me to make the plunge. The ladies make the market. And the men will spend whatever it takes to please them."

He looked at his watch. The interview was over. He stood up and shook my hand. "Oh, by the way," he smiled, "I might need a press specialist one day."

The Toy

He was a college professor who had gained credibility in worldly circles for his work on the behavior patterns of the human animal. It was a pleasure to talk to him. He was a man of some humor. Never above the crowd in speech or his research.

On this day he was looking at a sketch of a two-headed figure he had penciled on manila drawing paper. Before I could get a clear look he tossed it in a wastepaper basket.

I gave him a questioning look.

"There goes the perfect toy," he said. "It walks and talks and makes faces."

"Sounds like something any kid would go for."

"That's what I thought. I talked to the toy people about it. They loved the idea. I brought it to them. They agreed. Perfect for a child. They'd love it, age three to six."

His glum face lit up for a moment. "I tried it on the neighbors' children. They were ecstatic."

I nodded toward the waste basket. "So what's wrong?"

"It's a bust, yet they felt the kids would be crazy about it."

"So what's the problem?"

He shrugged. "'Yes, Professor,' they said, "'a toy any small child would love. But unfortunately kids three to six don't buy toys. Their parents do. And parents don't like anything that makes faces and has two heads—boy *and* girl. Too suggestive.'"

"Of what?" I put in.

He made a face. "Domestic disharmony."

The Decision Maker

At 35, he was a millionaire many times over. Known in the business world as the Boy Wonder. Nobody outside of the various companies he ran had a clue how he managed it. He didn't seem particularly smart. He had no family or social connections. In appearance, he wasn't prepossessing. He had a good growth of hair up front but not much in back.

I met with him in his office. It was casual. He only had the one secretary. She was attractive without being a beauty. He noticed my looking around the room.

"I don't like ostentation. It tells me the executive isn't sure of himself. He's doing a little dressing-up."

"It could also mean he likes to be comfortable in a pleasant surrounding."

"Then he should stay at home."

He sat back and looked at the clock. "So ask your questions. And then write what kind of a tycoon I am. That's the way all the stories go."

"I don't care so much about that. I'd like to know how you got there. You're my age."

He leaned back in his chair. "Very simple. At board meetings with these old duffers, everybody hesitated when it came to making a decision. I was the guy who came up with the answers. After a while they all looked to me like I was some kind of genius. They made me chairman of the board. And in time I had enough money to buy up the company."

I thought for a while.

"Did any of your decisions go wrong?"

He smiled. "Oh, yes, but by that time everybody had forgot who made the decision."

First Lady and the Cardinal

She was the first lady of a popular president. A personality in her own right. She wrote a daily newspaper column, lectured around the country, campaigned for political candidates and supported liberal causes. She was involved, and she was outspoken. There was no double-talk about her. She said what she thought and she said it clearly.

Her husband was long gone, but she marched on, doing battle with the conservatives and the reactionaries, not weighing the cost when she espoused a cause. She fought for the blacks, and the browns, the Orientals and other minorities. She was no stereotype. She decided each issue for herself. She belonged to a union, and was proud of it. But when she thought a strike was unfair, she walked through a picket line to make a talk which was pro-labor in its nature.

I had been assigned to cover her talk, and had questioned the propriety of her keeping the engagement.

She gave me a wry smile, discounting my youth in that glance. She spoke in a high, piping voice, without the slightest trace of an apology.

"What are *you* doing here?" she said. I could almost hear her say, Sonny. I felt the challenge in her voice.

"I am doing my job," I said.

Her smile widened.

"And that is what I am doing, *my* job. You may tell that to your readers."

And with that Eleanor Roosevelt dashed off on her next round of appointments.

The encounter had left me with a feeling of frustration. She had got the better of me, but in my youthful idealism, I felt she had oversimplified the issue. She was of the press, because of her column, but not in it or with it. She should have known that. I think she did. But she was of an aristocracy used to its own terms.

I thought of all this years later when she tangled with a prince of the church, thought by some to be second only to His Holiness the Pope in his power and influence in his church. The stories were all over the front pages. It was something any newspaper would eat up, a layman, and a lady at that, challenging the mighty Cardinal Francis Spellman, the Roman Catholic Archbishop of New York.

She had come out for Planned Parenthood, in her stated concern for the millions of hungry mouths around the world. She had advocated some form of birth control, stopping short of abortion. However, she had suggested that a woman had the right to manage her own body, as well as her soul. It was a controversial position then as it is now. But she was used to controversy.

She had been a loyal wife and a good mother. She had four sons, and though none approached their father's heights, they had done well in business and politics, and served their country with distinction in battle. She owed nobody an apology, not that she would have made one anyway.

The cardinal was outraged that a woman with such influence would take this position. He was so wrought up that he forgot for the moment who he was attacking when he charged that no fit American mother would take the stand she had.

Her answer was prompt and to the point. It was her feeling, she said, that she knew more about being an American mother, and what it implied, than her friend the cardinal. She carried the round with hardly a dissenting voice, for though the cardinal was an authority on many things, motherhood was not one of them.

To the delight of the newspapers, it looked like a battle was shaping up. But not for long. The first lady had nothing more to say, and the cardinal held his tongue. It looked like the fun was over, much to the disappointment of the press.

"She won't get within a mile of a reporter until this thing blows over," my editor said.

I had reason to think differently. I was friendly with her son Elliott, and had been invited for the weekend in the Hyde Park lodge Franklin Roosevelt planned for the retirement he never knew. Only a short walk from the manor house occupied by the first lady.

There were only a few of us on the weekend. We went for walks through the woods, down to the riverbank, and admired the sunset over the gleaming water. That evening we swapped stories over a barbecue. In the middle of the meal there was a long-distance call for Elliott. He was gone for what seemed forever, and was in fact almost an hour. He came back, shaking his head. The caller was a well-known publicist. "I don't know what he wanted," he said, "he kept talking about everything under the sun."

"Why didn't you break off?" I said.

"I thought it might come down to something."

He looked around and smiled. "Oh, by the way, Mother called. She's expecting us for lunch tomorrow."

His eyes stopped on me. "I told her I had a newspaper friend with me."

"I've met her," I said. "She won't remember."

He grinned. "Oh, yes, she does. She said, 'That brash young man tried to embarrass me.'"

"Perhaps I'd better stay behind."

"No, but nothing Mother says can go into the newspaper."

I had no choice. "No problem."

That night I had trouble falling to sleep. My mind wandered in circles. I thought of Franklin Roosevelt. He had been president so long that many young people didn't know any other president. "We have nothing to fear but fear itself," he told a nation that doubted itself. And that nation listened. He had done a lot of things people didn't like. But he had restored a nation's confidence and preserved a free world. And for that he would be remembered.

His wife carried on. She had been his eyes and his legs as she traveled the world, received with the same warmth that would have been shown him. For people had loved her even when they didn't agree with him.

I could hardly wait for noon to arrive. We walked down a short distance to the first lady's house. There were five in our party, including Elliott. She greeted us with her toothy smile and a warm handclasp.

We sat around and chatted for a half-hour before lunch. She was as I remembered her. The years had been kind. Aside from being a little grayer I saw no change. She stood erect, poised, with the same high voice, and the same assurance. She was amused by her son. It was heartwarming to see the gentle way they had of teasing each other. He mentioned the publicist who had talked so much without saying anything.

"I still don't know what he wanted, Mother."

She looked at him as if he was still a small boy.

"But of course you do," she said. "I am sure our newspaper friend saw through it."

I shook my head. With one phrase she had made me aware of my position.

"Why it's so obvious," she said, laughing at her son.

He answered good-naturedly. "Tell me, Mother."

"You just know," she said, "that he must have had a dozen people sitting around, listening, impressed with his casual conversation with the president's son in the home the president built." She gave her son a fond smile. "You really are naive, Elliott."

I saw immediately, knowing the caller, that she was right. She was a shrewd observer, and from her record, a loyal friend, and formidable adversary. She was conscious of her heritage, the responsibilities it entailed and the privileges it conveyed. She had been brought up in the White House by a president uncle who bore the same name as herself, and she was married in the White House to a future president with the same name. She was proud of what she had sprung from and saw it as an obligation to others less blessed.

She was superior, and made no secret of it. It put me off. With all her good points, I couldn't warm up to her. She saw people in their totality. In blocs and issues. She had no true compassion, I felt. Not for those who differed with her. And yet stood as tall in their devotion to a cause.

Her eyes were sparkling and I could see she was bursting with a story. "Before we sit down to lunch," she said, "I must tell you about an unexpected visit I had this morning. Indeed, my visitor left just before you arrived." Her glance swept the company, and stayed longest on me. "Of course, it can't be printed or talked around, not for now."

"You will never guess who my visitor was." Her eyes twirled around the room, and her laugh was gay and almost mischievous.

"Oh, Mother," pleaded her son, "don't leave us on tenterhooks."

She drew out the suspense a bit longer. "I got a call early this morning from a gentleman who said he was Bishop McIntyre. He was with His Eminence, the cardinal, and they just happened to be visiting some parishes in this area. And His Eminence would like to call and pay his respects, if it were at all convenient."

I could hardly believe that what I had looked for was about to be laid out before me, ironically, without my being able to do anything about it. That did not lessen my interest, nor keep me from wondering about a life pattern that suggested at times a synchronicity of events beyond coincidence.

She was delighted, she said. There was nobody she would rather see than her friend the cardinal. I was sure she meant it. For her agile mind had already conceived an idea that could bear unexpected fruit.

The cardinal and his coadjutor bishop came by in an hour or so and she served a mid-morning tea with crumpets and cookies. They went around the bush for a while, neither alluding in any way to the dispute that had exploded on the front pages. It would almost seem they were neighbors parted for a while, now happily rejoined.

I laid back, thinking little of note had taken place. But the sparkle in the first lady's eye told me she had something up her sleeve. Like her husband she had a flair for the dramatic.

She was pleased the meeting had gone well. For she liked the cardinal when she wasn't tilting lances with him. She didn't underrate him. She knew she was dealing with an adversary who militantly supported the causes of his church, and didn't know the meaning of retreat.

They had run out of pleasantries. Not once had mother-hood been mentioned. "The cardinal, lifting his skirts," she went on, "showed signs of getting ready to leave. He exchanged glances with his bishop [later a cardinal]. They nodded. The cardinal, half-rising from his seat, said politely if there was anything he could do for an old friend, he would be more than happy to oblige."

It was all the opening she needed.

"Yes, Your Eminence," she said, "there is something you can do for me." She smiled. "And for yourself as well."

I can just imagine how this was received by this mild-mannered man, who was sweetness and light on public occa-sions, with a sheath of Toledo steel under the pliant exterior.

"Whatever I can do," he replied, sitting back in his chair, with his wits about him.

"Oh, this is something you can do very easily," she said picking up on the qualification in his words. "As you know, our friend Governor Lehman had retired from politics when his party called on him to meet the challenge of a reactionary candidate. Ordinarily, his election to an important senate seat would be assured by his record, but a large element of the Democratic electorate is being weaned away from its tra-ditional party support."

She had his interest, but he was still unsure what she was getting at.

"Do you know," she went on, "that in many of your parishes, leaflets are being distributed on the steps of the churches advising churchgoers not to vote for the governor because of his veto of the school busing bill? I can assure you it was a difficult decision for the governor, and that it was a matter of principle he applied to all private and parochial schools. For, as he pointed out, the choice of a private school is the parents'. The public schools are open to all."

The cardinal was shocked. He was sure nothing like she described was taking place on the premises of his parish churches. "The church property is hardly a place for politics," he said. "Every Catholic knows that. I can assure you of that."

As usual, she held a trump card.

"I understand your disavowal," she said. "I would not have believed it myself, if I had not seen it with my own eyes. Please look into it, Your Eminence. I know you will be distressed."

I listened with grudging admiration to this old gut fighter. She knew how to go for the jugular with all the skill and adroitness of her late husband. She was by no means finished. She had not yet gained her objective.

She looked around our table and smiled.

"I had an idea the cardinal knew only too well what was going on. But I thought this a marvelous opportunity to help the governor who had done so much for liberal causes and the common people."

As the cardinal was puzzling over what she had said, she gave him something else to ponder.

"As you know," she said, with that saccharine sweetness she so often assumed, "Governor Lehman, as a Jew, will be far more ready than his Republican opponent, John Foster Dulles, a leading Protestant layman, to fight for minority causes in the senate. It would be well for you to consider this, Your Eminence, for the governor, you will find, will be your staunch friend as he has been in the past. You two have fought some good battles together."

Elliott asked the question we were all toying with.

"And how did the cardinal respond to this, Mother?"

She laughed. "He thanked me in the most gracious manner. He would consider everything I had said. We parted good friends, and good friends we are."

With this we all sat down to lunch, as I congratulated myself that I was not on the wrong side of this sweet old lady with the friendly smile.

The lunch ended without incident. I did not have anything to report, considering my pledge, but I did visit a few church steps in Manhattan, where I understood the pamphlets she mentioned had been handed out. I discovered they were no longer being circulated. As to be expected, without serious Catholic opposition the governor won the special election hands down and took his seat in the Senate.

I didn't think there was any prospect of my being invited back to lunch with the first lady, or even tea. There was nothing I could do for any of the many causes she championed. I was neither a cardinal nor a king.

Tin Pan Alley

*I*rving Berlin was the King of Tin Pan Alley. Song writer nonpareil and music publisher. For years his melodies and those of Cole Porter, Rodgers and Hammerstein, and Gershwin had caressed the airwaves. But, suddenly, as though a switch had been pulled, the sweet sentimental ballads were replaced by rock music amid rampant rumors of payola.

I called Berlin. He was indignant but cautious. "I'm not naming anybody, but we can't get our music on the air anymore. The disk jockeys won't even play my 'God Bless America.'"

"How about your 'Easter Parade' and 'White Christmas'? They've got to play them."

"They don't have to play anything. They control the airwaves. They play if you pay."

My favorite Berlin song was "Always." A sentimental song written by him as a young man to the young woman he was courting. She was the daughter of a wealthy magnate and he a kid from the Lower East Side of New York. The father locked his daughter in their luxurious home and kept the young lovers apart as the newspapers frontpaged this Manhattan version of *Romeo and Juliet.* Ellen Mackay in her isolation would turn on the radio and listen to the yearning lyrics of "I'll be loving you always, with a love that's always," and know her sweetheart was steadfast.

He told of his own lonely hours, with "All alone by the telephone, wishing and hoping you're all alone."

And now this music for lovers was stilled. And Irving Berlin didn't like it. "They don't even play Cole's 'Night and Day' or George Gershwin's 'Rhapsody in Blue.' It's all rock, rock, rock-around-the-clock."

He was a small man with a lot of fire. "Something has to be done. The music publishers are gutless. They should speak up. Music is a universal language. It speaks to all our people alike. We've got to keep this tenderness and love alive. It's what America is all about."

He was as eloquent a spokesman as he was a musical wordsmith. My story on payola created something of a stir. Berlin was quoted all over. In Washington and the Congress.

I decided he must be very proud of himself and the furor he had created. I hadn't heard from him but I imagined he was busy with congratulatory calls. He was a mover. He had set things in motion.

A week passed and I got a call. Our secretary announced with an impressed smile, "Irving Berlin is on the telephone."

He didn't bother with formalities.

"Your story was very upsetting," he said.

I was astounded. "Upsetting? I was careful to quote you correctly."

His voice was angry.

"That was the trouble. You did quote me correctly. But I stood alone. You said there would be others."

"They didn't have your courage."

"I told you they didn't have any guts." And with that he rang off.

Because of Irving Berlin, a Senate committee came to New York to investigate the payola scandal.

The words that brought them were Irving Berlin's. And the music. Who would think of "God Bless America," "White Christmas" and "Easter Parade" being silenced by the merchants of sleaze? Charges were brought, arrests were made. "Always" was back on the air, again part of the American language.

I wondered what Irving Berlin was thinking now. I waited for another call. It never came. I was all alone by the telephone.

Good Night, Sweetheart

"**M**usic is for lovers," said Jack Robbins, sitting down at his piano and pounding out a tune that even I knew was offkey.

"You got to give people music that puts them in the mood for love, no matter how old they are."

He was stocky and middle-aged, but he rattled the ivories like a teenager. It worked for him. He headed the MGM music division and had a perennial youthful look behind his thick glasses.

He went into another tune with the same vigorous assault on the keys. He obviously loved what he was doing, reminding me of Emerson's "Nothing is accomplished without enthusiasm."

I thought of my popular favorites. And when he came up for air, asked: "Do you know 'Good Night, Sweetheart'?"

He looked at me in mock amazement. "Do I know 'Good Night, Sweetheart'? Hell, I wrote it."

"You wrote it?"

"Well, not exactly. Let's say I helped Ray Noble with it. One of the few bandleaders who could write a tune you could dance to."

He proceeded to stand up, and with his arms circling an imaginary dancing partner, did a little waltz around his parquet floors.

He ended his dance with a flourish, humming "Good Night, Sweetheart," as he went back to the piano. A light came into the twinkling eyes as he traveled back over the memory years.

"Yeah, we were sitting around, just like we are today. Ray was showing me his song. I was playing it, thinking it was good, but there was something missing. It was a great song. But it hit me wrong. And then it came to me. It was too downbeat."

"It didn't seem that way to me," I said.

"Of course, it didn't. I fixed it. Here's the way it went originally." He looked over his shoulder as he beat on the piano. Singing in a voice that must have given its gentle English composer the shakes.

"Goodnight, sweetheart, sleep will banish sorrow."

He looked over at me triumphantly.

I shook my head. "That's the way it went when Noble's band played it."

"Not so. There's a line missing. Don't you see? The way I just played it, the guy says goodnight, and tells the girl sleep will banish sorrow. It's more like a goodbye than a goodnight. Sorrow. Obviously they had a fight. So that's the end of it. She has to sleep it off if she can. And what about him? So what kind of a love song is it?"

"So what did you do?" I said, not remembering all the lyrics.

"What did I do?" He was appalled. "Didn't you go to college? The song closed every college dance."

He sang it again in his unforgettable voice, a sort of whiskey baritone.

"Goodnight, sweetheart, sleep will banish sorrow."

And then pausing, his head cranked over his shoulder, his voice booming, adding the line he'd dreamed up . . .

"Goodnight, sweetheart. *Until we meet tomorrow.*"

He repeated the line, then stood up with a happy grin. "Do you get it, kid? Tomorrow. They quarrel. Then they make up . . . Tomorrow. A happy ending. That's what we need, happy endings."

He was right. There couldn't be too many happy endings. If only tomorrow.

A Movie Connection

Adolph Zukor was one of the Hollywood patriarchs. Along with Samuel Goldwyn, Louis Mayer, Jesse Lasky, the Warner Brothers and William Fox. He was the board chairman of Paramount Pictures. Even a brash, younger Joseph P. Kennedy wasn't about to displace him when he came out to Hollywood to run Paramount studios. But he did give him a good nudge or two.

Zukor was in his 90s. He looked tiny behind his giant desk. But he had a ready smile and the laugh of a man who still found life amusing.

"Did you say you were from *Confidential*?" he said, mentioning the notorious scandal magazine that had torn Hollywood celebrities to shreds.

"*Newsweek*," I said.

"Oh, *Confidential*," he repeated, cupping his hand to his ear with an elfish smile.

I started to repeat myself, thinking he was hard of hearing, when I saw the twinkle in his eyes. Zukor was having his fun. I was sure he had been a match for the granite-jawed Kennedy in the Hollywood power struggle.

I could see he was studying me. "You seem like a nice young man," he said. "What is your interest in Mr. Kennedy?"

I shrugged. "I was sent out to do a story about a controversial figure whose son could be president. They say the apple doesn't fall far from the tree."

A faint smile touched the thin lips.

"Talk to Gloria Swanson by all means. They did a movie together. *Queen Kelly*. It only cost her $300,000."

My eyebrows went up.

"Oh, yes, Joe got her to finance the picture. He's a very persuasive gentleman."

He shuffled some papers on his desk, and checked his watch.

"Oh, yes, call Miss Swanson. A wonderful lady."

I turned to leave. He was cackling to himself when the door closed behind me.

I had seen Gloria Swanson in a comeback movie about a silent film star in decline. *Sunset Boulevard*. It was a great picture, with Bill Holden. The kind of picture you don't easily forget. She played herself. She was brilliant.

Over lunch I told her I had admired her performance. She seemed pleased. She was smaller than I thought, petite, still attractive, with eyes that changed color in the sunlight. She was the center of attention in the restaurant. And very aware of it. She enjoyed the spotlight.

She had brought her lunch. She explained, with an apologetic inflection of her throaty voice, "You know, we all poison ourselves with processed foods. White sugar, white flour, white salt. The three deadly whites."

She proceeded to bring out an organic whole wheat sandwich, with sprouts and tomatoes and lettuce sticking out from the edges of the bread, and went about the interview in a placid way.

"I wouldn't do anything to hurt Jack Kennedy," she said.

"He's a friendly young man. So there's very little to say."

She had a greater concern.

"I'm concerned about the food they're giving young people. It's making them juvenile delinquents. All that sugar, it makes them violent."

I remembered reading where people with hypoglycemia, low blood sugar, were sometimes diagnosed as manic depressive and psychopathic because of the *sugar blues*.

She nodded emphatically and bit into her sandwich.

"Until we stop feeding kids sugar, we got more than the Kennedys to worry about."

The Patriarch

He was as controversial as anybody could be, and still stay alive. He was rich and powerful, a diplomat who was anything but diplomatic, outrageously outspoken, ruthless and arrogant, said to be a racist who had given comfort to the Nazis during the war. His son, a congenial personality, seemed his opposite, but his adversaries were quick to point out that the father would be pushing the buttons. "Elect the son, and you'll get the Old One, too," they said, "in spirit and the flesh."

At the convention that nominated the son, his enemies slipped leaflets under the delegates' doors, reinstating the ugly rumors of the father playing footsie with the Nazis when he was our ambassador abroad and sympathizing with their views about the Jews who were their victims. The candidate had taken pains to privately distance himself from his father. But he could not run privately, nor could he disown his father publicly. It was a dilemma.

There was a saying you could judge a man by his enemies. He seemed to have more than his share, picked up as he danced lightly from a fortune made on Wall Street into such varied enterprises as real estate, merchandising, movies and booze. He succeeded in everything he attempted, leaving a trail of blood and tears in his wake. He was a bad man to be related to if you were running for the presidency. He knew this. He was concerned with what his connection might do to his son's chances. Above all things, he was a realist. He often said:

"I made my fortune knowing what I was dealing with."

He knew what he was dealing with now. It was for a greater prize than he had ever known. For his son's election would be a consummation of his own dreams, and a redemption of the prejudice he himself had known in his native city. It was something he wanted more than anything in his life. He had to be discreet, yet make it clear he was not the ogre he was painted. And, at the same time let it be known his son was independent of him.

He did not beat around the bush. He knew what needed to be told. "I am not anti-Jewish," he said flat-off. "I've beaten the Jews in various businesses they excel in, Wall Street, motion pictures, whiskey, real estate, merchandising. I have nothing to envy or resent them for. That's what anti-Semitism is all about. People who can't compete with the Jews look around for reasons to get back at them. It doesn't matter how trumped up these reasons are.

"Most of these guys are losers. Look at Hitler. He never made it at anything until he discovered anti-Semitism, and got a lot of other losers like Goebbels, Ribbentrop, Goering and Himmler into it with him. All together, the whole bunch couldn't have run a hot dog stand.

"I have nothing to apologize for. I know what prejudice is like. For years I was 'That Irishman' in my own city of Boston, where not too long before there were Help Wanted signs that said, 'No Irishmen or dogs need apply.'"

He did not speak in anger. It was too late in the day for him for that. It was as though he wanted the record cleared once and all.

"My political mentor, Barney Baruch, was a Jew. He was the adviser of presidents, a man whose roots went back to the Confederacy. With his help I became head of the Security Exchange and the Maritime Commissions. General Sarnoff of RCA and Adolph Zukor of Paramount were colleagues. The man who runs what you reporters like to call my 'vast empire' is a Jew. Isadore Kreisl. I even belong to a Jewish country club. The only gentile. Does that sound like what they say I am?"

No, it didn't, but the winds of gossip blew strong and would not be stilled.

"There were reports that you were sympathetic to the Nazis when Hitler was stepping up his persecution of the Jews."

He spoke as a man sure of his convictions, who had nothing to hide or dissemble.

"I was the English ambassador at the time. The president had recalled our envoy in Berlin, and had directed me to do everything I could to ease the plight of the oppressed in Germany. I would have entertained the devil himself if it meant helping one victim of the Nazi terror."

"Also you used the offensive expression Sheenies in talking about Jews?"

He laughed. It was a booming laugh.

"I plead guilty. I told the Irish at a St. Patrick's Day dinner they should behave with greater dignity. They booed me. All my life I have called Italians Dagoes, Poles Polacks, Jews Sheenies, and the Irish Micks, and sometimes Donkeys when I didn't think they were particularly bright."

Did he still talk this way?

His eyes lit up in a smile.

"Not until after the election. And then I can't promise anything. It's hard to beat back the habits of a lifetime."

At a time when England stood alone against a victorious Hitler, he said the English were through and it was sending good after bad to help them. There had been an outcry at home, and he lost his post. He blamed it all on a reporter who had not allowed for his well-known flamboyance.

"The hometown reporters knew I was talking off-the-cuff. They didn't quote me. This guy was on a journalism fellowship. He was hoping to make a name for himself. I won't tell you what that name is. It wouldn't be polite."

I couldn't help but laugh. "Are you criticizing him because he quoted you correctly?"

"He knew no diplomat could talk that way and remain a diplomat."

There was another reason for his abrupt departure from the London scene. The English had complained that the protocol of the Court of Saint James was demeaned by the Ambassador's insistence on presenting a lady friend at court.

The president had called in some temper.

"Joe, I want you to get rid of that woman immediately."

And Joe had answered: "I'll get rid of my mistress, Frank, when you get rid of yours."

He was an achiever, and achievers give a reporter something to write about. He had attained more than any business figure since the last of the robber barons. He was richer than some Rockefellers, and owned more Manhattan real estate. He had a corner on the best Scotch and owned the biggest merchandise center in Chicago. He had controlled three motion picture studios at one time and lived like a star. When other millionaires were going broke in the 1929 stock market crash, he was laughing up his sleeve, making new millions selling short in a down market after cashing in before the collapse.

I couldn't help being amused by some perfectly human
foibles he had. He didn't like the racetrack particularly, but
he had bought one to inflate his image. He knew nobody
could beat the horses, not even him. He would quietly bet a
two-dollar ticket on every horse in the race, then produce the
winning ticket for an admiring female companion, and say
with a modest smile, "I had him."

He had managed the real estate affairs of his church and
made so much money for the church doing it, that he began
doing it for himself. He had gone into the whiskey business,
with the blessing of a president of the United States, on the
promise of a lucrative job for a presidential son. The job never
materialized. He put a lifelong friend into his whiskey business, promising him a large share of the sale price when he
sold the business. Instead, he offered a few thousand dollars
and another job when the sale was made for millions of dollars. It ended the friendship. And though the disenchanted
friend wound up with another whiskey concern, the resent-
ment still smoldered.

I met with this friend in his home on the Cape. It was a
comfortable place, cozy, but nothing fancy, just a trot from the
ocean. He was a grandfatherly looking man with genial blue
eyes that lacked the steel of the Old One's, and a paunch that
spoke of good living. He spoke softly, without rancor.

Ever since he could remember he had been with the
Ambassador. He ran a business for him, or an errand. He
baby-sat the kids. It was all in the day's work. Sometimes he
was the court jester, the butt of the Ambassador's razor-
edged humor. He would squirm with embarrassment. Always
inside. For he was counting on The Promise, the pot of gold
at the end of the rainbow to secure his declining years. At the
same time, knowing his man, he tried to get The Promise in
writing.

"He would smile that toothy smile of his and say, 'You have nothing to worry about. Trust me.' I thought of the people who had trusted him and I had nightmares. 'Suppose something happens to you,' I'd say. He'd give me that smile again and say, 'Don't give it another thought. The boys will take care of you. They know about it.'"

The years had mellowed him. It wasn't as important as it once was. "It was the broken pledge that bothered me. I don't think I ever expected to get the money. It would have been out of character."

Old Joe's obsession with the presidency intrigued me. He seemed more caught up than the candidate. I wondered when the presidential bug first bit him.

"It goes back to having all those doors closed in his face. There were clubs he couldn't walk into and it rankled. He wanted to be a trustee of Harvard and they wouldn't give him a nod. He couldn't even get an honorary degree. That's why he wanted the White House. He wanted it first for himself. He thought he could do it better than any of the chumps in there. That's how he thought about them. Chumps. But the time wasn't right. Not for a Catholic. He had backed the first Catholic for president, Al Smith, and he saw what they did to him. He was trounced by a man nobody knew. So he groomed his boys, step by step, concentrating always on the oldest, waiting for the right time. He knew it could come. Just like he saw the Depression coming. The Catholics were getting stronger, but they needed other minority votes if they wanted to elect a president. He saw that the Jewish votes could be decisive in key states. He had nothing against Jews. He used them like he used everybody else. Everybody was the same to him. So many pawns to be moved around at his pleasure. He didn't care what a man's race or faith was. Unless he was of English extraction. He'd had enough of that thrown in his face. He fired an Irish lawyer who was running things for him, and hired a Jewish lawyer in his place. He didn't like people getting too important. There was only one indispensable person. You know who that was."

He chuckled to himself. "I used to tell him, 'God bless any one of your sons who becomes president. They'll have to answer to you.'"

"Do you really believe that?"

"Naw, Jack's just as tough as he is, he'll take what he wants from Joe, just like Joe always did. In that way they are alike, but the resemblance ends there."

I made a detailed report for a cover story on Old Joe. It went to the top editors, and they batted it around for a while, deciding to put the final version into the hands of an editor who knew more about group journalism than I did. I would have probably started it off, newspaper style, telling the readers what we thought so important, about Old Joe and his prejudices. That wasn't the way it went. I was given the final version to check over. It began with the Old Joe on first base, in college, batting .300. That meant he got one hit out of every three times at bat. Not bad for an Irish kid bent on making a million dollars before he was 25. My head was bobbing in acknowledgment of the editor's adroitness when I got to the halfway mark, and almost jumped out of my chair. There was the word Sheenie, just as Old Joe had spoken it, spelled like he would have spelled it. Taken by itself, out of context, it offset everything I had gone to such pains to determine. There was nothing to indicate this was a manner of speaking, however offensive, that he applied to other groups. I thought it should be in context or deleted. The top editor, Denson, was off on a pre-election holiday. The assistant filling in was pleasant enough, but Ivy League cool. A Harvard elitist of a circle Joe could never crash.

"What's the problem?" he smiled. "All we're saying is what you said he said."

"Without clarification the tone of my report is contradicted with one word. It will not hurt the father like it will the son. It's not fair."

There was no expression on his face.

"As it is," I said, "I cannot stand behind the story."

Shortly before the copy deadline an aide came to my desk. She, too, was cool. "I am to notify you the deletion has been made."

Two months later there was an election. With Joe's arch-enemy, Lyndon Johnson, as Jack's running mate. Old Joe's son triumphed by a razor's edge, amid rumors the father had won over several states where the politicians were properly approached.

Old Joe called two or three days after the election. There was a happy ring in his voice.

"I think my son will make a great president," he said. "I wasn't so sure at first. We were talking Cabinet, and I mentioned a Wall Street investment banker of a conservative bent for the Treasury post. At that, Jack's face got red, and he exploded. 'Let me remind you,' he said, 'that you were not elected president of the United States.'"

That bothered Old Joe. He left the room in dismay. The next morning the son looked him up and apologized. "'I'm sorry, Dad,' he said. 'Tell me more about this man.'"

Joe was elated. The man he recommended became a key member of the cabinet. But it was Joe's Last Hurrah. He sent me a note explaining his position. "I can no longer do the things I would like to do," he wrote, "like a book attacking Lyndon Johnson, now that I am the father of the president."

Presidential Suite

I saw an announcement by the White House that President Kennedy had acquired a special office and workplace in New York City. Out of curiosity I made a visit to the penthouse apartment in the Carlyle Hotel. I was taken to a top floor of this fashionable East Side hostelry by a hotel guide, and permitted to inspect the president's Manhattan quarters.

The hotel was well-run and well-situated in a neighborhood favored by a number of political celebrities, such as Mrs. Eleanor Roosevelt, the widow of the four-times President. The suite itself was disappointing. It didn't look like anything a President would want to spend a great deal of time in.

The rooms were small and cramped, so unlike the White House, that I wondered how the president could be comfortable working in so confined an area. There was a small living room, a small bedroom, a small kitchen and a small dining area. It didn't go with the picture I had of a privileged president with a rich father. And homes in Hyannisport, Massachusetts; Palm Beach; New York and suburban Washington.

It remained a puzzle. All you could say for it was that it was probably a good place to rest the presidential head away from the fury of politics when in New York. Presidents like Hoover and Truman had made the plush Waldorf-Astoria Towers on Park Avenue their home away from home. But they were more ceremonial and older than this young and energetic president.

I gave it no more thought until I got a call one afternoon from a female reporter whose job it was to cover the president for the Hearst Washington bureau.

She was in Boston with the presidential party and had been planning to enplane that afternoon for Washington. She had informed me of her plans only that morning.

"Perhaps we can have dinner this evening," she said. "His nibs has changed his plans and is stopping off in New York. He has business there."

"Ah," I thought, "the presidential penthouse does serve some purpose after all."

"What kind of business? Is it classified?"

"It's classified, all right," she said. "He's stopping off to see his girlfriend."

I had heard these rumors so long they no longer interested or tantalized me. And this particular name had been mentioned more frequently than any other, including Marilyn Monroe's.

"So where does she hold forth?"

"On the fashionable East Side. In an apartment at East 76th Street and Madison Avenue. Across from the Carlyle Hotel."

Kennedy's Friend

"I've got a luncheon date with somebody at NBC," said *Newsweek's* top editor. "I want you to come along. He says he knows you."

That somebody was Al Rylander, a network vice president in charge of everything.

"Do you need a witness?" I said.

John Denson grumped and looked at his watch. "Get a move on. We're late."

We arrived at the restaurant on time. And waited. And waited. Denson had one coffee, then another, his face darkening with every tick of the clock.

"I don't know what this guy wants. He called me. He must want something."

"Yeah," I agreed. "It's amazing how they can restrain themselves when it's helping somebody."

Rylander finally arrived, out of breath and apologetic. "Sorry, something unexpected came up."

"It must have been important," Denson said.

Rylander nodded.

"It won't go any further?"

Denson shrugged. I didn't say anything. I was just along for the ride.

"I was on the phone with Sandy Vanocur. You know him?" He looked at Denson. Denson inclined his head a sixteenth of an inch.

"Sandy's our White House man. He's traveling with Jack Kennedy in California. Kennedy's stopping at Peter Lawford's beach house in Santa Monica. You know, the English actor married to Jack's sister?"

I could see Denson's eye flicking around for a waiter. He wasn't terribly interested.

"Yes?"

"Anyway Sandy was griping about not getting as much money from NBC as David Brinkley and some others."

"'I should be getting top money,' he wailed. 'I'm covering the top man.'"

"You're not only covering him," Rylander said, "you're covering up for him."

"What do you mean by that?" Sandy came back.

"How about their smuggling this actress into Lawford's house for the president in a sailor's uniform."

"How did you know that?"

"Certainly not from you," Rylander said.

We could tell from Rylander's smile that he knew who the actress was. It wasn't Marilyn Monroe with whom the president's name had been linked. Not somebody that well-known. But still a star and a blonde.

The luncheon moved on without incident. Rylander talked in circles. Denson was his grumpy self. I could see him frown. His mind was elsewhere. The president's frivolities didn't interest him. He was debating what to put on the cover of the magazine. The weekly deadline was here.

We climbed into a cab, Denson still grumping.

"I don't know why that guy's complaining. They wouldn't have used it if he'd reported it. They're doing the same thing Sandy did. A coverup. Why blame him? He has to stay on the good side of the White House."

A puzzled look came over his face. "You know, I still don't know why Rylander called. Do you have a clue?"

I shook my head. "No, but we know why he was late and Sandy won't be getting a raise."

Lady of Pleasure

She didn't look any different from any pretty cheer-leader who wore saddle shoes, bobby-sox and a sweater that jumped up and down when she did. And yet there was no mistaking why she had been standing around in a busy street. And why I had been assigned to interview her.

I knew where she lived. It was hardly Park Avenue. I dropped off the taxicab, and went on foot the last few blocks to work off the uneasiness building up inside me. As I idled along now I saw two or three young women in doorways. They looked up and smiled. I didn't smile back. I didn't want to connect them with the quiet blue-eyed girl I was going to see. The street was bleak and bare, not a tree or a bush on it. The people in the street looked defeated, crawling by without meeting your eye. In time I came to a dingy building with the right address. The faded yellow brick front was cracked in places, showing its mottled seams. The front door was crudded with old paint. The stone steps slanted at an angle. The place looked like it was ready to fall apart. I walked up one flight, sniffing the odor of old plaster. A rickety railing trembled under my hand. The number she had given me was etched on a door in a back hallway. I rapped twice, gently, then harder. The door opened an inch or two, then enough for me to step in sideways. She was holding herself together in a thin wrap. She had just gotten up. Her hair was in disarray and she yawned, showing two even rows of pearly teeth. She didn't say anything. She led me down a dark hall into a dark living room. The shades were drawn. It looked as if daylight had never touched the place. She switched on a lamp. In the dull light I made out the drabness of the carpeting and the furniture. The upholstered chair she gave me had a broken spring. She slipped into a small love seat which had seen better days. I looked around for a moment. On the wall there were a number of prints that didn't go with the rest of the place. They were old English carriage prints of horses and the elegant men and women who rode them. She had followed my eye. "Those are mine," she said. "Everything else is the landlord's. But the bed."

From where I sat I could look into a room with a large bed and a lace-fringed canopy over it. It looked rumpled, and I wondered whether it had been recently engaged.

"I don't receive *anybody* here. This is my retreat."

She seemed annoyed.

"Where do you go on *assignment*?" I said. It sounded silly as I said it, but it was the only word that came to me.

She shook her head, stretching out her hand.

"I get paid first. For talking."

I pulled a hundred-dollar bill out of my wallet.

She looked at it, turned it over a couple of times and put it in a metal box.

"My hope chest."

She looked at a cheap clock over a gas-burning fireplace.

"You're paid up for an hour. Now to answer your question. I'm a hotel girl, but it's always a suite. Or there's always the home, if the loving family is away."

There was a bite in her voice. She didn't seem like the girl I had encountered on the street 24 hours before. I thought I had seen a quiet appeal in her eyes then. I guess I put it there.

She got up and mixed a couple of Scotches.

I shook my head. "A little early in the day for me." It was scarcely noon.

She downed one drink, then another, making a face. The whiskey seemed to pull her together. She reached for a cigarette, settled back in her seat and crossed her slim legs.

"What is it you want to know?"

I had not expected her to be so matter-of-fact. It caught me short.

"You don't seem the kind of a girl . . ."

She cut in. "That's what they all say, like they're sitting in judgment."

She no longer reminded me of a cheerleader. I looked at her closely. Without makeup her skin was pale and sallow, the sweetness was gone. She was attractive, but in a different way.

She crossed her bare legs every time she took a puff on her cigarette. It was distracting. I could see what men saw in her. And why they paid her. She seemed aloof, untouchable, yet she was available for a price.

She poured another Scotch and again she grimaced. She didn't like the whiskey, only what it did for her.

A hundred men had asked her what I asked. It was all I could think of. "How," I tried again, "did a girl like you . . .?"

She yawned.

"The world is made up of would-be sociologists," she said with disdain. "I tell them all the same thing." She gave a tired sigh. "It's the usual story. I was date-raped when I was 16. He was a college man. I wanted him to think I was grown-up.

So I kept drinking until everything got hazy. He took me to a motel where they rented rooms by the hour. I didn't know what happened until I woke up. He was gone. I never saw him again."

It sounded like something out of a soap opera.

"I can't help it," she said, "if life is bad television."

"It takes two to tango."

Tears came to her eyes. I had touched a raw nerve.

She sprang to her feet and paced the floor. The words poured out of her. "What do you know?" she cried. "Do you know what it feels like to be treated like an animal?"

She stopped in the middle of the floor and gave me a look that seemed to reflect every abuse and indignity she had suffered. "Do you know what it's like to look in a mirror and hate what you see, and know it will never be better?"

I knew of women who had been raped and had pulled themselves together and led productive lives. It had taken some doing, counseling and prayer, deep searching into themselves, but they had managed. They had not gone on the street.

"It's not too late. You're 19. You can move on. You have your youth and beauty."

"My youth and beauty?" She flung back at me, throwing herself onto a couch. "I have to take myself with me. Don't you understand?"

She pointed at the wall. "See the crack in the plaster? That's where I banged my head the night I became a whore."

She pulled back the sleeves of her wrap. I could see the scars on her wrists.

"I tried to kill myself, but God wouldn't let me die. And in sparing my life He gave me something to live for."

It was a curious remark, but I didn't think about it until later.

She stood up abruptly.

"You'll have to excuse me," she said. "I have to see a man about a horse."

She disappeared into the bedroom. When she returned her eyes were bright and she did a little jig, humming along with it.

"Cocaine?"

"Heroin," she said with a dreamy look. "Horse. It keeps me broke."

She looked over at the clock.

"That reminds me. You owe me another hundred."

I took another bill out of my wallet. I had three left. I wouldn't need them. There was only so much anyone could take in any one day. Even a reporter. She took the bill and put it with the other in the metal box.

A cat I hadn't noticed before came out of the darkness and jumped onto her lap. She stroked it a few times, murmured a few words of affection, then settled it back on the floor.

"I had her fixed when I had myself done," she said with a laugh.

She leaped from one mood to the next, jaunty one moment, depressed and angry another. The drugs and the alcohol may have had something to do with it, but mostly I felt it was something else, something festering inside.

What you are, a wise man once told me, is what you do. I wasn't so sure of that as we sat together almost knee-to-knee. Obviously, she didn't like what she was doing. And who she was doing it with. At times, when she was unguarded, I detected a softness in her, a sweetness brimming on the surface.

But how did I get at it? I decided I would appeal to her sympathies. I had been told prostitutes liked to help the downtrodden and the underdogs, as that was how they saw themselves.

"You know," I said, "if I don't come back with a story I'll be in trouble."

Her eyebrows raised.

"You mean you might lose your job?"

"You can never tell," I said, which was not exactly a lie. Not even the soothsayers knew all that the future held.

She frowned.

"Tell me how I can help you."

As it had been from the moment I met her, the big enigma still was how a girl like herself had become a prostitute. One incident of rape on a date seemed hardly enough to bring on a cycle of self-destruction.

"I'd like to get into your background, your childhood. Somebody once said, 'Give me the boy until he's six, and you'll know the man.'"

She permitted herself a bleak smile.

"I'm hardly a man."

I could see her mind going back. Her eyes clouded over and I saw her hand tremble. It was slight. Yet it said something. What, I wasn't sure.

I said casually, "Did you have brothers or sisters?"

She shook her head.

"I was an only child."

She wet her lips and gave me a searching look.

"You said there would be no names?"

I nodded.

"Your father and mother, were they together?"

"My father deserted when I was born. He couldn't handle a child. I had a stepfather."

She looked away as she mentioned her stepfather.

"How did you get along?"

She laughed, but there was no laughter in her voice.

Whatever it was, her memories, the drugs, the alcohol, a remarkable change took place. Her face became that of a small girl, her look piteous and entreating, as though seeking help and understanding. I listened, mesmerized as she relived that childhood. Her voice that of a child. She stammered, fumbling to express herself.

Observing the downcast eyes, the trembling and tears, was like partaking of her agony. I felt like a Peeping Tom, held in the grip of her horror. Not once did she mention her stepfather by name. It was always *he*. Her voice fell to a whisper.

"He told me never to tell Mommy because she would send me away. Every night after Mommy fell asleep he would come to my room and lie down next to me, and play with me under my nightgown. Sometimes he would take it off, but only when Mommy was out of the house. He told me it was something I had to do, that fathers did this with their little girls so they would know about love when they got old enough to marry."

She buried her head in her lap and started to sob. I put my arm around her. She drew away with a shudder.

"I was only ten," she cried. "Ten years old."

The emotion that drained out of her drained me as well.

I felt a pang as I listened to her sobbing. She seemed to symbolize everything that was wrong with our world. The abuse of children, the indifference of people wrapped up in their own concerns, the lack of guidance. And, above all, the lack of love. It was so easy to say that she was young, and her life stretched ahead of her. And yet it would never be easy for her. There were scars that never healed; scars others never saw or cared about. She had to live with what she had become. I had to remind myself that I was a reporter, not a sociologist or a man of the cloth. And then it occurred to me that perhaps in telling this broken woman's story it might help others by bringing attention to the cracks in our culture in a way that would touch the human heart. Ironically, I still had a story to get. But she was more, a shattered young woman who needed more than I could give. For in her eyes, the male animal had become the enemy.

The anger and frustration spilled out of her as she stopped her sobbing, and wiped the tears from her face. "It wasn't just my home. It was everywhere. It was always the same. When I left home and came to the city the cab driver had a hotel to take me to. The bellhop had people he wanted me to meet. When I went for a job, they wanted to know why I wanted to be a secretary when I could do 10 times as well dropping my skirt."

Her eyes flared and then went dead. "I don't know why I'm telling you all this. You don't give a damn, except for your story."

She sat back, depleted. She had an unhealthy pallor. And her breath came in gasps.

"You need to take care of yourself," I said. "You should have regular checkups."

She frowned and looked away. She knew what I was saying.

"I don't see doctors. There's no need for it. I know what I have to do."

She was so fragile, so helpless. How could she strike back at the rich and the famous, the influential men who gave her the money for the alcohol and drugs she needed to face herself in the mirror?

"There is nothing you can do," I said. "You're outside the law. You're the one who pays the piper."

A smile crossed her face.

"I have a way," she said, "a woman's way."

I was puzzled, not seeing what she was getting at. And then I saw the look of triumph in her eyes.

"You wouldn't dare?"

"Oh, yes, I would." She laughed. It was not a nice laugh. "Why do you think I never go to the doctors?"

She got up and did her little jig. A one-step a child could have managed. She fell back into the love seat, and her eyes bored into mine. Defiantly.

"They have it coming to them," she cried. "They gave it to me. I'm giving it back."

A Blueprint for a President

*C*olin Powell for president? A bemusing thought.

As the popular Joint Chief during the U.S. military excursion in Iraq, he had become an American byword and a familiar face. And with the Republican victories in the elections of 1994, his face had reappeared in dozens of magazines and newspapers. With a big question mark after it. Would he be the inevitable outsider to make a run for the White House?

Nobody knew at the time. But it was a provocative thought. Powell had nothing to say. He was a modest, unassuming general, and generals weren't the run of politicians. Grant and Eisenhower had done it, both military heroes, capturing the White House. Powell had stayed behind the lines, directing the Middle East conflict from the Pentagon, but the victory was as much his as anyone's.

But was this enough? Not quite, according to another Joint Chief, the redoubtable General Omar Bradley, ground commander of American troops in Europe in the onslaught against Germany in World War II.

As with Powell, the name of General Douglas MacArthur,

the hero of the Japanese war, had once been bruited about for president. At the time I was interviewing Joint Chief Bradley, World War II had been over for some time, but the haloes of the conquerors were still bright.

"What kind of a president do you think General MacArthur would make?" I asked Bradley in the presence of an aide.

He frowned, then replied. His answer off-the-record, a condition that no longer applied with the passing of the principals, Bradley, MacArthur and subsequently Eisenhower.

"No one has a greater admiration and appreciation of General MacArthur than myself," he said. "He was largely responsible for pushing Eisenhower and myself to the forefront. Without his sponsorship we may never have attained the commands we ultimately had. The fact remains that all of us were trained in the military, for battle roles, not peace roles. Trained to be soldiers, commanders of troops, knowledgeable of military tactics and strategy, and to take battle stations in the defense of our country. Anywhere that confrontation took place. We weren't schooled in the art of diplomacy, in peaceful negotiation, or maintaining the balance of power. All statecraft. Not military craft."

MacArthur, some thought, was of larger dimension. Hadn't he ruled a vanquished Japan with the wisdom of a Roman proconsul? So fair-minded and farseeing there were many in that subjugated nation who admired him.

"Oh, yes," smiled Omar Bradley. "They were used to an iron hand. They respected it. But this was a defeated nation, not a free, democratic nation like ours, which is traditionally jealous of its freedoms. Not that MacArthur would have trod on these freedoms. But his first reactions to a threat against these freedoms, nationally or internationally, might very well have been of a military turn. He was trained to keep the peace, not make the peace."

It all sounded very plausible. And how about Eisenhower, the loveable Ike, Bradley's immediate superior in the European conflict, and his classmate at West Point? The two almost inseparable over the years in thought and action.

"It might be even more of a problem for Ike. He doesn't have the background of civil administration MacArthur had in Japan. He has a more volatile temperament. On the other hand he might not be as arbitrary. More subject to the influence of civilian aides, thinking they knew more about the various civilian departments than he did. He would be fair. But he would still think in any emergency like a soldier first. It would be only natural."

I thanked him and his aide, an old friend, for being so candid. And I never dreamed the time would come with the passage of events that I could honorably record this great general's opinions as a historical footnote.

I had occasion to smile to myself, reflecting on this interview, a few years later when Eisenhower, then president, warned the invading forces of our Allies—England, France and Israel—to get out of the Suez Canal zone owned by Egypt or else. They got out, no doubt remembering how some 10 years earlier the Allied troops led by this same Eisenhower had made an unprecedented invasion of the European continent to break the back of the vaunted German military machine. And end a long war.

Apparently a military background, in the name of peace, could cut both ways. And who knows but what General Powell could manage it?

The Cab Driver

I picked up the cab on 52nd Street, just off 5th Avenue. It was midnight. Manhattan traffic was beginning to taper off.

"Where to?" said the driver as he flung open the door. He was bright-eyed and youthful looking, with an amiable smile.

I mentioned an address in East Harlem.

He gave me a doubtful look, then lurched away from the curb and headed uptown. I could see him look into his rearview mirror. His curiosity finally brimmed to the surface.

"What's a white man doing in that neighborhood after dark?"

"I'm a reporter," I said, thinking that would settle it.

"You're still white."

I laughed. "I'm going to a rap session where they try to get kids off drugs."

He turned his head a little, with one eye on the road, and gave me a smile.

"That's something. We need more of that, people working together."

We seemed to be hitting it off, so I thought I'd ask a few questions. I liked cab drivers. They were the voice of an embattled city.

"So how do we come together?"

He shook his head. "That's a tough one. It's got to come from inside. Whites don't like each other, so why should they like blacks? Every day I hear white people, sitting where you're sitting, badmouthing Jews, Italians, Polacks, Armenians, Catholics whatever they're not. So why should whites care about us?" He laughed. "I never hear anything against blacks. I guess they're afraid I'll run them into a pole."

He made more sense than any of the great liberals and pundits I'd been listening to. He was a realist, without the liberal viewpoint unclouded by fact. I thought I'd try him again.

"So what can be done?"

I saw him frown into his mirror.

"Nobody's going to help the black people but themselves. We got to see more blacks who made it giving blacks jobs. That's where it is. Economics and pride. We got to help ourselves. It'll give us a lift. Take this cab. I'm driving for somebody else. Someday I'll drive my own. Somewhere."

He cranked his head around with a smile. "Who knows? Maybe I'll have a fleet before I'm through. And a few jobs to give out."

I'd gained something of an education. Looking inside the outside. I gave him as big a tip as my purse would allow.

"Maybe you can buy a wheel with that."

We'd stopped in front of a dingy building on East 116th Street.

"Thanks," he said. "Tell it to those kids like it is."

"Just like you," I said.

War and Peace

Though approaching 80 at this time, the Countess Tolstoy was a sturdy-looking figure with a strong face and a no-nonsense manner. I liked her immediately.

In her impeccable English she asked what I did. I mentioned I was a writer.

She smiled. "So was my father."

"Yes," I said. "All by himself."

I mentioned a book I had just read about him. A look of disdain came into her eyes. "The man had no idea of what my father was about. He read what other people had written with the same lack of insight. The result was a lack of understanding compounded a dozen times."

She gave me a challenging look. "What do you think was my father's deepest concern? The war against Napoleon, life among the Russian nobility, the struggle of the serfs?"

I thought a moment. I had been invited to this upstate New York settlement to view a model farm based on the great Russian's ideas about farming. I had no idea she was in charge of the project or would even be there. She was his youngest and only surviving child.

Everything I had ever read or thought about Tolstoy was going through my mind. *War and Peace, Resurrection, Anna Karenina*, the *Power of Darkness*. The great novelist always searching, always grappling with the mysteries of life and death.

I could see her looking at me, waiting. I wondered why. I was not a famous figure, not anyone known to her. And yet we had formed an instant rapport.

"These things you mention," I said finally, "strike me as being related to his search for the meaning of life. In *War and Peace* and his other books there was a preoccupation with man's existence. Life and death were not very far apart to the characters who struggled through his pages. At times death seemed to be an obsession. It was as though the two were irretrievably interwoven. I had an idea he may have believed in reincarnation."

She looked at me in surprise. She hadn't expected anything like this. And neither had I. I didn't know where it came from.

She studied me for a moment as though trying to remember where we had met.

"Very interesting," she said. "And what is your feeling of why we are here, scurrying about like so many ants?"

I smiled. "You mean all of us? Or just some of us?"

"Yes, from the former Czar of all the Russias to the lowliest peasant."

"I think we're here to find out why we're here."

Her eyes thrust at me like twin arrows. She nodded thoughtfully. "Yes, here and beyond."

She looked around at the milling crowd, and her look took in the friends who had brought me.

"I would like to invite you all to lunch. So we can talk. You are still a young man, and yet I have never met anyone with the understanding you have of my father."

I could see a tear in her eye. In a moment she collected herself. "Let me tell you a story about my father. He was my whole life. He still is. I was 26 when he died, his youngest daughter, and the only one in the family to stand with him when he decided to collectivize his estates for the benefit of the workers.

"I was with him when he died. It was as if part of me had died. I stayed in my quarters on my father's farm and wept until there were no tears left. I was inconsolable. For days I didn't eat or sleep. I didn't want to live. I was tormented by thoughts of joining him. Then one evening in the midst of my despair my father's disciple came to see me. He loved my father and my father thought of him as his son. I sat up and tried to compose myself. He took my hand and held it for a moment. He spoke in a soft voice. I thought he was about to console me, and I was afraid I would burst into tears. His words took me by surprise."

"Your father would be disappointed in you," he said. "He would not like you grieving like this. He thought that you, of all people, would know his feelings."

She straightened herself in her chair and looked at him in wonder.

"He did not believe death was the end. You, his dearest child, should know that. Death, he wanted me to remind you, was the reality. Life the unreality. Sing no sad songs for him. Rejoice in his deliverance."

With a surge of emotion she stood up and embraced this man her father loved.

"Yes," she said. "I know. I have been foolish. I have thought only of myself. I miss him so."

"He is with you. He shall always be with you."

She bowed her head. "And I with him."

I was deeply moved, near tears myself, when she stood up

and took my hand. "Now for lunch with our friends."

The lunch passed pleasantly, my friends agreeably surprised by the Countess Tolstoy's hospitality.

After lunch, as the others were preparing to leave, she
drew me aside.

"We have not finished. I have been waiting for some time
to talk to someone about my father's books. And see them
published again. Books like *The Kreuzer Sonata*, which had
no wide acclaim, and his private papers and thoughts about
many things." She gave me a direct look. "Someone who
understands my father. Would you be interested?"

I was overwhelmed. So much so that I didn't say anything
for several moments.

"I know little about publishing. But I would consider it a
great honor."

I gave her a questioning look.

She understood. "My father stipulated that no author roy-
alties were to be paid on his books after his death. This
should make them available at a lower price for more people."

I didn't see this as an obstacle. After I had recovered from
my surprise I thought about how I would go about justifying
her confidence in me, protecting her interests and preserving
the good name and reputation of the world's greatest novelist.

My mind turned to the man who protected my own interests with publishers, and had done a good job of it for years.
I decided the countess and her father would be happy with
him. He was knowledgeable, prestigious, honest, without
artifice, and like myself would be gratified at the thought of
so noble a mission without thought of compensation.

I had known Sterling Lord for years. We had done a dozen
books together, tilting lances with publishers from time to
time, and we had never lost a battle. He looked just right to
me.

He had a certain dry humor. I thought I would tickle it a little.

"How," I asked, "would you like to represent Leo Tolstoy?"

There was a long silence.

"Leo Tolstoy?"

"You know, the man who wrote *War and Peace*."

There was another long silence. I had an idea Sterling may have thought I'd been imbibing. I proceeded to explain.

"I'd be delighted," he said.

I could see by his tone that his appreciation of my talent was rising by leaps and bounds.

With some elation I telephoned the Countess Tolstoy. "It's all set," I said. "I got the best agent in New York to get the best publisher for your father's books and papers."

There was a deep silence. I sensed a change in her voice.

"This was not how I saw it," she said. "You were to get them published. You understood my father so well. It was a very personal thing. Between us."

I explained I knew nothing about drawing up contracts and the legalities entailed in the protection of a writer's interests.

She said, "I understand." I read the regret in her voice as she rang off.

I was disappointed. I had an empty feeling. I sat and looked at the phone. I would have liked to pursue it any way she wished. But now the spell was broken. I would never know why she had turned to me. Nor why my interest in Tolstoy had been so strong ever since I read *War and Peace* as a boy.

I mentioned my disappointment to a friend, telling him how badly I thought I'd handled things.

He smiled and shook his head.

"Your problem was elementary," he said. "You understood Tolstoy. But you didn't understand his daughter."

PART TWO

Books and Mystics

The Great Maya

I found the Great Maya without too much trouble. She was sitting at a corner table in the lounge of a Manhattan supper club, close by the restrooms for Ladies and Gentlemen. You couldn't miss her. It was the shank of the evening, so to speak, and she was alone. She was a pleasant-looking, dark woman, middle-aged, and the way she was shuffling her playing cards you could tell she had been doing it for a long time.

As I walked in I saw her look at me, but moved on to the restroom when an imperious voice stopped me. It was the Great Maya.

"How about a reading, big boy?"

"What kind of a reading?"

"About your past, present and future."

"Oh," I said. "A fortune teller," and turned away.

She half-rose from her table. "I am not a fortune teller," she said, in a metallic accent. "I am a sensitive."

She gave me a piercing look.

"I know what's bugging you. You have just gone through a divorce. You have two children to show for the marriage, the boy's the older, isn't that so?"

I stood staring at her. The place was empty. I had dropped by on the spur of the moment.

"Sit down," she said, "and relax. You're all knotted up."

I sat down across the table from her, watching as she put the cards away. "I don't need them," she said. "They're to concentrate with."

She talked about herself, just enough to let me know she was no ordinary person. She was from an island of witches and she had the gift of second-sight. "I see behind the veil of time. I tell people what I see, good or bad." She had been telling them for 30 years.

"I don't bother with trivial things."

"Why can't you pick the horses?"

She gave me a pitying look.

"A newspaperman should have better questions."

It gave me a start. How did she know that? I wasn't the kind of reporter you saw in the movies. I didn't wear a hat with a press card in the band nor did I have a cigarette dangling from my mouth.

I felt something stirring uneasily inside of me.

"How did you know I was a newspaperman?"

She gave me a lazy smile.

"You poor boy. What do I have to do to make you believe?"

I threw a bill down on the table.

"How about one of your readings?"

She pushed the money away and closed her eyes. Her lips were moving. I leaned forward to catch what she was saying. Her voice appeared to have undergone a change. It was deep-throated and husky, with a slight tremor. Her eyes were open now and glassy.

"Not too long off you will leave the newspaper and become a writer of books. You will write about the metaphysical and other things. But it will be for the metaphysical you will become known."

I had no idea what the metaphysical was, nor did I think for a moment I would be doing what she said. There was one question of a personal nature on my mind. I had seen enough of what she could do to toy with the idea of putting the question to her. What could I lose?

She was waiting, her face more relaxed and softer than I had seen it.

"Do you see me marrying again?" I said, as casually as I could.

She gave a little sigh.

"You are planning to be married even now, but she is not for you. You will be spared. You will never see her again."

I felt a shiver down my spine and said in a tight voice, "What do I owe you?"

She folded the bill that was on the table and handed it back to me. "I want nothing from you."

That evening, with a hand not quite sure of itself, I dialed the number I had not called for weeks. The gentle, soft voice I knew answered with a sweet hello. But there was a quietness, a lack of spontaneity.

"I don't know how to say this," she said, "but there is something I must tell you . . ."

It was not necessary she say any more.

That was our good-bye. I never saw her again.

As a reporter I believed in what I could touch, taste, see and smell. My friends were amused by my new interest. One of them, a bit of a *bon vivant*, scoffed when I mentioned the Great Maya. He was some years older than myself and assumed a paternal posture.

"That woman is turning your head. Drop her before you become a zombie."

It gave me pause. And then another of her predictions materialized. A publisher had read one of my features in the *News* and wanted to develop it into a book.

I was still not a believer, but I wanted to know more about something I didn't understand.

My friend, Waltham, was dismayed.

"I'm going along with you," he said, "and let that woman know she must stop playing around with your mind."

I was not sure I wanted him there.

"You must have an engagement. Please don't break it for me."

Waltham always had an engagement. He was married, but he required more than one woman for diversion. He had no idea of what he was doing to his wife. He took silence for assent.

I had spoken to him about it. He would only shrug and say, "Leave it to me, Sonny. I know what I'm doing."

He insisted on joining me one evening. When we arrived, the Great Maya was in consultation. She signaled that she would be but a moment. Waltham looked at her with a derisive smile. "So that's the great one. She looks like she should be scrubbing floors."

I told him to cool it. He had been drinking. "Go down to the bar and I'll join you in a few minutes."

He would have none of it. "You don't get rid of me that easy."

The Great Maya's client left, and we sat down across the table from her. I introduced Waltham and his Southern gallantry with the ladies came to the fore. He acknowledged the introduction with a courtly bow.

I told her about the book offer, and she gave me a pleased smile. "There'll be a third book," she said. "That will be a bestseller and enable you to do your own writing. Then you will write about the metaphysical." She gave a little self-disclaiming laugh. "And about me. And what I have told you."

Waltham had ordered a drink at the table. He downed it with one gulp and looked at her out of bleary eyes.

"What are you doing to this boy?" he said. "He was a normal young man till he met you. Now he sounds like some kind of a nut."

I tugged at Waltham's arm with a sinking sensation in my stomach. I saw that Maya's dark eyes were flashing and the color had come to her face.

She looked Waltham in the eye. "I'm not used to being spoken to like this. If you have nothing better to say I wish you would leave."

"I'm not leaving. Not till you stop poisoning this boy's mind." He gave me a pitying look. "The poor boy actually believes you can see the future. He's bewitched."

He leaned forward as if he was about to tweak her nose. "You don't look like a bad person, so cut it out before I put a hex on you."

He broke into a spasm of laughter, slapping his hand down on his knee. "That's a good one," he cried, "hexing the hexer."

There was nothing I could say or do to stop him. I looked at Maya. Her face was aflame and her eyes snapped. All the pent-up fury of a proud woman broke loose.

"You dare to hex me," she cried. "Well, Mister Smart, I will hex you."

I looked at Waltham. He had become strangely subdued.

Her voice rose in a shrill crescendo.

"You've been getting away with murder, cheating on your poor wife. She's going to leave you, my friend. And when she does all your fine ladies will mean nothing. You will be a broken man. You will plead and cry but it will be too late."

Waltham's face was the color of parchment. His head had cleared, but fear lurked in his eye.

She was not through.

"You will move out of your home. You will drink more and more. You will wind up in a fleabag of a hotel and spend your last days there. Sooner than you think." Her eyes flashed with scorn. "Now hex me, if you can."

I was shocked, it had happened so quickly. I looked at Waltham. He had gotten up and said with a dash of bravado, "My wife will never leave me."

She turned from him in disdain, and walked out of the room. We sat looking at each other.

I couldn't put her words out of mind. We never discussed the incident. It stood between us whenever we met, until he stopped seeing me. He disappeared out of my life. He didn't answer my calls, and his wife was vague. They had broken up. I didn't know where he was. Six or seven months later I got a call from his wife. She was sobbing. She had found him in a cheap hotel. He had been dead for two days. He had lived there the last few months, in a tiny room, with a bathroom down the hall.

"Poor Waltham," she cried. "He was the only man I ever loved."

The Kennedy Curse

*C*omposer Alan Jay Lerner of *My Fair Lady* and *Camelot* fame called to make a psychic evening of it with Jean Smith, nee Kennedy. Could I produce a psychic on short notice?

I was not surprised that he turned up with the president's sister. He had been with Jack Kennedy at Choate and Harvard, and knew the family well.

Jean had the inquisitive intelligence of the Kennedy clan, with a striking resemblance to brother Bobby. As we chatted before dinner I noticed her running her eyes over my bookshelves. I got up to remove a book of mine that had foreshadowed the president's assassination. She saw my move and held up her hand.

"I know what I'm looking for. I know the page."

She picked the book out. It was *The Door to the Future*. She gave me a bleak smile. "We checked on this psychic. We found she was right 10 percent of the time."

The dinner was a success, but I could see Alan wondering where the psychic was. "We'll have to cab over to a Madison Avenue hotel," I said. "Only a few blocks."

The psychic, Mary Talley, was finishing up at another table. She was heavy-set and pleasant-faced. She moved with difficulty because of her weight. She sat down and flipped out her cards. She saw nothing in them. It was a way of focusing her concentration. She looked up and smiled. I could see she had recognized the two immediately. Jean would have been identified as a Kennedy anywhere, and Alan's success on Broadway hardly qualified him for anonymity.

"I don't want any of you to tell me anything," the psychic said. "We'll see what we see."

Alan gave me a suspicious look.

"I haven't said a word. I didn't even mention your prison record."

It was a joke.

She started with Alan. He had been married eight times. She tuned into this activity with an uplifted eyebrow. When she touched on his closeness to the Kennedys he darted another look at me.

I shook my head.

"Yes," he acknowledged, "I was talking to Bobby Kennedy only a few days ago. He wanted me to join him riding the rapids in some forsaken place like Idaho or Montana."

"Are you going?"

"I told him it was against my religion. I'm a born coward. I wasn't going out of my way to break my neck. 'Riding the rapids at your age,' I said. 'Are you trying to kill yourself?'"

"And what did Bobby say?"

Alan hesitated a moment. He looked at Jean. She didn't seem to notice.

"Bobby said it didn't matter what he did. He was going to get it in the neck anyway. 'There's a curse on this family,' he said, 'so I might as well do what I want to do. While I can.'"

Alan made an effort to speak lightly. But a pall came over

the table. I looked at the psychic. Her face had become solemn. She said under her breath so only I could hear,

"Some things can be changed. But not all."

I thought of this the night Bobby was assassinated in the kitchen of a Los Angeles hotel. His guards had chosen a devious route to protect him from attack. He had been running for the presidency. There was little doubt he would have made it had he lived.

Some things changed. But not Bobby's words. He may have been more psychic than the psychic. He was a fighter, living on the cutting edge. He could have made a difference.

The Matriarch

I marveled at the tranquillity of this woman who had suffered so much. She was 90 years old at this time and there was not a line in her face. Her cheeks held their youthful bloom and her eyes were clear and bright. She had a shy smile and a way of cocking her head to one side like a bird.

Her faith and her New England staunchness had helped her carry on as one blow after another befell her family with the finality of a Greek tragedy. One daughter born retarded and another an airplane casualty. The first son, the most promising, killed in battle. The second son, a president, assassinated in his prime and a younger brother who aspired to succeed him meeting a similar fate. Only one was left now of the four sons pointed almost from infancy for the presidency.

And this was Teddy Kennedy, a United States senator like his brothers Jack and Bobby before him. There was talk of Teddy running for the high office, challenging an unpopular president, Jimmy Carter, for his party's nomination.

What, I wondered, as we sat in a quiet corner of a Palm Beach hotel, must pass through a mother's mind at such a chilling prospect?

She had kept in the background, avoiding the spotlight that appeared to devour her family. I was surprised at this break with the past. When I mentioned how I admired her courage she gave me a shy smile, blushing like a 16-year-old told she was the prettiest girl at the high school prom.

She soon made her interest clear. "You know many psychics, I am told," she said. "And what they foresee."

"Oh, yes," I laughed, "but I don't know if I'd set my watch by them."

"Some, I understand, are quite accurate."

"True," I said, "but it's often hit and miss."

She mulled this over.

"Have they made any predictions for the next election?"

"For the presidency?"

She nodded.

"There have been some."

Our eyes met.

"And what do they see?"

I hesitated. I knew what the psychics were saying, but I had no idea how accurate they might be.

"Mostly," I said, "they see one man."

"And his name?" Her head was poised now like a frightened bird's.

"Ronald Reagan. They seem to agree on him."

She smiled and thanked me. There was no change of expression in her face. And yet I sensed her disappointment. As she moved off, I marveled again at her composure. She had the faith that moved mountains and reached deep into her soul.

I almost wished I could say the name began with a *K*. Like the fortune-tellers do when they're not all that sure. But I was sure. For a dozen psychics had forecast a California president with a double *R* in his name.

Phil Donahue

Whenever I had a book to promote I stopped off in Dayton, Ohio, to chat with Phil Donahue on his little show. He was always genial and friendly, the best talk show host on the circuit. Always the right question, to highlight a subject, probing yet pleasant. Always playing fair, never laying back and tricking the unwary. Always trying to bring out the best, so his audience would have the best.

His only problem was that he was in Dayton. Not that there was anything wrong with Dayton. It was a delightful town to visit and live in. But it wasn't big-time television, and that's what Phil Donahue wanted more than anything in the world. I could see it in the dispirited way he sat in his cubbyhole of an office after a show that went well. He was no farther ahead than before. He was still in Dayton.

I was in Chicago, scheduled to do a network show, and discovered at the last minute it would mean canceling the Donahue show in Dayton. A foul-up by the people handling the tour.

"I can't cancel Donahue," I said. "So you might as well plan on getting me to Dayton in time for his show."

The groans could have been heard in Dayton and New York.

I forget the flight plan. But I got booked on a small plane that reminded me of the Toonerville Trolley, then switched at some point to a helicopter, and landed in a barnyard outside Dayton an hour before showtime, knowing I was to do a show in Minneapolis that night.

The show was a success. It couldn't be anything else with Donahue. Later we had coffee in his little office. I could see the same lurking unhappiness I had seen so many times. I sympathized. He was a big-town guy in a small town.

"You know, Phil," I said, "I write about the psychic, and we talk about it on your show, but every once in a while I see something myself."

He looked up without much interest.

"I see you with the biggest talk show in the country. On the NBC network. You will be amazed at your success."

"Thanks," he said, with a polite smile.

The years passed. I no longer got booked into Dayton with my books. Phil Donahue was the talk of the TV world. His shows, with the audience participating, were like a breath of fresh air. Instead of the usual hot air. I rejoiced in his success and thought no more of it. Until one day I got a call from the publicity chief at Bantam Books.

"I don't understand it," the man said. "Phil Donahue wants you on his show with your book *Soulmates*."

"What don't you understand?"

"He doesn't get into the metaphysical. It's not his cup of tea. I asked him why he was getting into reincarnation and all that. All he said was that he wanted you on with the couples you wrote about."

I laughed to myself. "So he finally talked you into it?"

Somehow we made it to Chicago. Three *Soulmate* couples and myself, with a large studio audience, and millions on the tube.

Before the show went on Donahue took me aside. "I never forgot your canceling that network show in Chicago to do my little show in Dayton."

I was touched.

"It does you credit. So few remember."

It was the high spot of the show for me. Everything else was anticlimactic. I didn't even mind when some lady in the audience stood up and brandished her fist at me, saying, "All you're in it for is the money."

She was partly right. I was appearing to help sell my book. And an old friend, Phil Donahue, was helping.

Johnny Carson

"Johnny Carson must like your book," said my Doubleday editor Lee Barker. "He called in from vacation and told his staff he wants you on his show as soon as he gets back."

I groaned. Carson was hardly a fan of mine.

"I was on once before. He told his people not to put me on again. I talked too much. What can we expect?"

"Just don't say anything," he laughed, "and make sure you hold up the book to the camera."

The book was *Edgar Cayce the Sleeping Prophet*. It had been at the top of the bestseller list for weeks, and now Johnny Carson was getting around to it. There was something rotten in the air somewhere, and it wasn't Denmark.

"I think I'll pass."

Barker's face dropped. "We spend a fortune on our publicity department and we haven't had an author on a major talk show in two years."

I sighed to myself. Lee Barker was not only my editor but my friend and mentor.

"Okay," I said. "You owe me a dinner."

The night of the show I was accompanied to the television studio by Dick Boehme, a Doubleday aide. The first stop was the show's talent coordinator. As he sat across a small desk from me, I sensed his uneasiness. He seemed to be having difficulty meeting my eyes.

"You won't mind," he said apologetically, "if Johnny goes over you a little? Nothing personal. Makes for a good show."

I wondered if his conscience was bothering him. He seemed like a pleasant-faced, honest young man.

"I don't mind," I said. "I'm a man of reduced expectations."

I turned to Dick Boehme. "It looks like a rocky evening."

He smiled. "Think of the sales."

Waiting to go on, I sat entranced in the monitor room hearing myself lauded time after time as a great journalist and bestselling author. I leaned over and whispered in Dick's ear. "The big buildup before the fall."

A turbaned figure crossed into view on the television screen, making a series of ridiculous predictions as the studio audience applauded and burst into laughter. His name was the Karnac the Magnificent.

"Now who could that be?" I said in dismay.

"Johnny Carson," Boehme said. "Funny, isn't it?"

The signal came. I was to go on next. After me there would be a dancer or a singer. I wasn't sure which. It seemed academic.

I came on with the usual fanfare of music. And Applaud signs. And was immediately confronted by a smiling Johnny. He held aloft a copy of my *Edgar Cayce the Sleeping Prophet*, and half-facing me and the audience said, "Aren't you surprised that people read this kind of stuff?"

I had been expecting something of this nature.

"Not after that remarkable exhibition of yours."

The studio audience burst into a gale of laughter. I could see Carson's start of surprise.

I had the first round.

He was a seasoned campaigner. He kept coming back with one jab after another. "Now your man Cayce," he began.

I held up a hand. "He's no more my man than anyone I investigate. . . ."

"And so how did you conduct your investigation of a man who poured forth all this marvelous and astounding information while he was asleep?"

"It was like fishing for herring in a barrel. Everything he said was transcribed, and put down in triplicate, so there was no chance of altering a prediction or a diagnosis to suit the event."

"You write this man was able in trance to diagnose the illnesses of people he had never seen, and prescribe remedies that cured them. Is that not right?"

I nodded. "Yes, I checked the results with dozens of people who had consulted him as a last resort and been cured."

We had been batting it back and forth, running through a performer's time. I had no idea how it was going. But I could tell from its reaction that the studio audience was absorbed.

During a commercial break I got my first inkling of why Carson had asked for me. In his disarming way he said, "You know, my wife [wife number one, Joan] and her mother are interested in Edgar Cayce. They're members of a Cayce study group."

It made me wonder. A husband bashing an interest his wife held dear. It hardly seemed like connubial togetherness.

The break ended and the show resumed.

Carson had an unmistakable look of satisfaction on his face. He was ready for the kill. "Considering that Cayce was an illiterate, a sixth-grade dropout, as you say, how could he have possibly described the human anatomy in such detail as you say and prescribe complex remedies unknown to skilled medical people?"

I could sense the expectancy of the studio audience in the hush that followed. I had heard the question many times and had asked it myself.

"There is only one possible explanation," I said. "Everything else has been excluded." I paused and looked him in the eye. "Edgar Cayce had the hand of God on him."

There was a moment of silence, then a thunderous burst of applause from the audience, and the program ended almost as though on cue.

Freddie de Cordova, the show's producer, leaped forward and shook my hand. "That's one of the best shows we've ever had. You'll be on this show often."

I knew I would never be on the show again. And I never was. I guess I talked too much.

Note: Joan and Carson were divorced. Joanne followed. Then Joanna. Then Alexis.

Tammy and Jimmy Bakker

We were discussing a book together at a time when evangelist Jimmy Bakker was being accused of defrauding the faithful of millions with phony promises of a paradise retreat.

My eyes shifted from Jimmy to Tammy, then back again. "The only way I could do this book would be for you to make a clean breast of everything. Throw yourself on the mercy of your flock and ask for forgiveness."

I could see Jimmy hesitate. But Tammy nodded with a bright smile.

His lips tightened. "I haven't done the things they say I did. I have enemies in the evangelical ranks like Jerry Falwell and Jimmy Swaggart. They're bent on destroying me."

"Why would they want to do that?"

He shrugged. "It's rather obvious."

"You mean they're rivals?"

He nodded. "They'd do or say anything to discredit me."

I had watched a program on the Larry King television show where a youngish minister said flatly that Jimmy was a homosexual. I didn't find it significant, but obviously the

minister thought it was a deviation that made Bakker unfit
to serve his God.

"Are you aware of this minister's statement?"

Jimmy nodded. "Yes, it's part of the plot to discredit me by
the Falwell-Swaggart group."

"I don't think this minister had any connection to Swaggart
or Falwell."

"Not on the surface perhaps."

"Have you denied the allegation?"

He shook his head. "There wouldn't be any point to it.
They'd get some wino to trump up some wild charge that I'd
propositioned him in a steamroom. People would believe
what they wanted to believe."

"I heard it was a sauna."

"You see," he said, "it changes and grows in the telling."

"People might believe you if you dealt with it openly. And
might then disbelieve anything else that you handle up front."

Tammy had been following the conversation closely. She
was still smiling. "I think it's a good idea to get everything
out in the open. I think people will respond to that."

I looked at Jimmy. He was composed and unmoved. He had
a way of talking as though his eyes were glued to the Bible
and his heart mounted on the Ten Commandments. I could
understand why the faithful had flocked to his church of the
air. He was their channel.

"I don't think it would do any good," he said, "to get into all
the phony charges leveled against me. It would only give
them more attention than they already have."

I looked at him for a moment and sighed. We were sitting in
the desert home of a friend who had thought enough of the
Bakkers to think they could stage a comeback. I wasn't so sure.

"Are you saying that you are completely innocent of the
fraud charges brought against you?"

"I am saying it would do no good to deny anything. My enemies are influential and powerful enough to produce as many witnesses as they need to say I did the things I didn't do."

Tammy's smile disappeared. I had the feeling she was doing what she thought best for her husband. My interest in the book disappeared with her smile. The fraud charges were repeated in court and Jimmy went to prison.

Tammy was not implicated. I saw her picture in a magazine with another man. They looked very happy together. She was doing her own channeling now.

Profits for Prophet

She had trashed *The Fountainhead* only a week or two before. On its 25th anniversary. It was one of the more compelling novels of our time. So I didn't see what chance a book like my *Sleeping Prophet* had particularly when it was about Edgar Cayce and psychic phenomena, which so many people didn't believe anyway.

"Oh, see her," said my editor, "a story in the *New York Times* can't help but do you good, whatever she writes."

She seemed like a pleasant enough young lady. Her name was Nora Ephron. As I recalled she had written that the Ayn Rand novel didn't have one favorable review when it came out. An irate publisher had turned around and taken an ad in the *Times* reprinting the original *Times* review which had indeed praised the book.

She went on the attack early, criticizing the psychic books of Ruth Montgomery, a former colleague of mine. One being *The Gift of Prophecy* about psychic Jeanne Dixon.

"She's obviously in it for the money, wouldn't you say?"

I had worked on the same paper with Montgomery for years. I had no qualms about her integrity.

"No, I wouldn't say," I responded. "Please remember it was you who said it, not I."

She moved on undismayed. She mentioned the Edgar Cayce Foundation, which promoted the psychic readings of America's greatest psychic, and enrolled members all over the world.

"I've heard," she said, "that the Cayce people are making a good thing of it."

She obviously felt a newspaper story wasn't newsworthy unless it took somebody apart.

"I don't know where you got that," I said, "but again it's your opinion. Not mine. So please remember that."

She went on to another book I had done. *Yoga, Youth and Reincarnation*. Which I had written after studying the various postures of this Oriental discipline with a number of teachers. Like *The Sleeping Prophet* it had been quite successful.

"Do you still do the exercises?" she said, measuring my tall, angular frame with a glance.

"Oh, yes, it helps keep me fit."

There was a little more desultory conversation. And she left. I assumed that was the end of it. I hadn't said anything that would make it worth a story in the *Times*.

I was wrong. There was one target I had overlooked. Myself.

I saw the heading first. "Profits for Prophet." Of course she hadn't written the headline, or maybe she had. She was quite versatile. As to my yoga, she hadn't been impressed. I didn't look as if it had done me any good. Except perhaps in the wallet.

I heard no more about her. Then years later I was watching a movie I enjoyed. *When Harry Met Sally*, featuring Billy Crystal and Meg Ryan. In the screen credits was the name Nora Ephron. She had changed professions. She was the screenwriter. I was happy for her. She had found a couple of people she liked. Even if it was only a movie.

Cicely Tyson

"**I**s it possible," said Cicely Tyson, "for someone to crawl into your mind without your being aware of it?"

"Some psychic people do," I said, wondering at the question and her obvious anxiety.

She was a person I admired greatly. Her towering role as the ex-slave in *The Autobiography of Miss Jane Pittman* was unforgettable. Her screen portrayal in *Sounder* was a classic. But above all I admired her warm inquiring nature and her courage in adversity.

Yet here she was, troubled, trying to collect her thoughts, plainly nervous and ill at ease as she fidgeted in her chair.

"I'm frightened," she said, "and I don't know where to turn."

We were friends and neighbors and discussed the metaphysical from time to time. I had an idea she had come to me because of a book I had done on the subconscious mind, a book she had read.

I smiled, trying to be casual. I had never known her to be anything but upbeat and relaxed. She was the one person, I thought, who knew who she was and where she stood.

"Shall we start from the beginning?" I said.

"If I can find it." She sighed. "I saw a story in the paper about the mother of the two Spinks boys. It described how she had struggled all her life to encourage them and see they got an education. And now they were fighting in the same Olympics, the first brothers to do so, and she didn't have the money to go to the games to see them make history. I wanted to do something about it."

It was *Sounder* all over. Cicely had lived the role, the hardworking mother who struggles to raise a family and get a son his education. And now she was reliving it.

She paused as though to think her story through.

"I had this overwhelming desire to make this mother's dream come true, I knew how she must feel at this moment of triumph. I didn't want to appear patronizing. So I had to think about how to go at it. The family lived in St. Louis. I scouted about for the address, meanwhile weighing the different ways I could help. I finally got it worked out."

The troubled look returned. And the sigh.

I waited. And she went on.

"I received a letter from the mother, thanking me for what I had done, expressing her appreciation and that of her boys. They were touched, she wrote, that someone of their race they admired so much would take the trouble to think about them and care."

How wonderful, I thought.

"You should be proud of what you have done."

She rose from her chair.

"You don't understand," she cried. "I didn't do anything. The letter arrived before I could do anything. That's what frightens me."

I looked at her in disbelief.

"You hadn't mailed or wired the money, then forgot?"

She shook her head. She had stared at the letter, reading

and re-reading it. Turning the envelope over in her hand. Examining the postmark. Her confusion grew as the Spinks brothers (later to be world heavyweight champions) went on to Olympic titles.

"Your name was on the envelope Mrs. Spinks mailed?"

"I was in a play at the time. The letter was addressed to me, 'Backstage, New York.' And I got it."

"Did you mention your intention to anyone?"

"No, that would have spoiled it. I didn't want anyone to know."

She looked at me with a face full of wonder.

"How could somebody do something in my name, knowing better than I what I wanted to do?"

I strained for an answer.

"It could have been somebody like-minded. Somebody who read the same article you did. Somebody who admired you, somebody who had seen *Sounder*, and empathized as you did. Picking up your thought."

She shrank back in horror. "That's what bothers me. Somebody tuning into my mind. Able to twist it in some evil way if they so desire."

I now understood her uneasiness. It was as though you'd come home and found a thief had rifled through your private belongings. Everything you treasured. Only this was worse. Invading the privacy of the mind.

"There are ways of protecting yourself. Opening your mind to positive thoughts. Through the process of visualization and meditation described in the course I took while doing my book."

Her face lightened for a moment, though still doubting.

"Where can I take such a course?"

"Oh, there's a number of teachers."

She was eager now. "Can you recommend someone?"

I thought about it. Somebody she'd be comfortable with. Somebody convenient.

A name came to me, as though out of the blue.

"Dorothy Nelson. I've sat in her classes. She's down to earth and dedicated."

"Where can I find her?"

The last I'd heard she was living nearby in Southern California. I had no telephone number. I tried Information. There was no listing.

I shook my head.

"I haven't seen her in months. I have no idea where she is." I smiled. "Maybe we can visualize her."

The phone rang. I picked it up. It was Dorothy Nelson. She was driving across the country to her California home and had a sudden impulse to call.

"We were just talking about you."

She was not surprised.

"Naturally."

Cicely's eyes widened.

"There's somebody who wants to talk to you," I said into the phone, handing it to Cicely.

"You see how it works," I smiled. "We send out our thoughts. And, boom, she calls."

It was not always that simple.

But it worked this time. Cicely took the course.

The Courier

t was a Monday and traffic was light. As I was about to turn off Hollywood Boulevard, I saw a boy standing on the corner hitching a ride. He looked 13 or 14. His thumb was in the air and there was an appealing look in his eye. He had a shoulder bag strapped across his chest. I could see the bag bulging at the bottom, like a kid delivering newspapers.

I stopped and he climbed in.

"Where you bound?"

"Hollywood High," he said in a choir-boy voice. "Do you know the time?"

"Three o'clock or so," I said, not having a watch on me.

"I've got to be there in time to make my deliveries."

I nodded toward his bag. "What do you have there, newspapers?"

He pulled back a moment and gave me a long look. "You a cop?"

I laughed. "I was a newspaper reporter. That's as close as I came."

I'd stopped for a light. "You haven't told me what you got in that bag."

"You still a newspaper reporter?"

I shook my head. "No, I'm working on a book."

The bag had opened enough so I could see he didn't have any newspapers. Whatever it was lay buried deep in the cloth bag.

He seemed very nervous. "I got to get to the school before classes are out."

"Meeting friends?"

"Some are."

Every time we stopped for a light, his eyelids started to twitch.

"On Mondays," he said, "the kids get their allowances. I got to get there before they go off and spend it."

We were drawing close to the school.

"You didn't tell me what's in that bag."

He leaned over and whispered. "The best pot money can buy. Acapulco Gold."

His eyes were shining now. "Have you tried it?"

I shook my head, wondering how I'd been so dense. "I don't do drugs."

We were a block from the school.

"I'll get off here," he said, peering down the street. "Thanks for the lift." He smiled. "Try it sometime. It'll give you a lift."

My eyes followed him as he moved on. Classes were letting out. In a few moments he was surrounded by exiting students. And digging busily into his bag.

I couldn't help wondering how much Acapulco Gold and Panama Red he sold that day. And what it did to the kids who bought it.

Note: My book came out. It was called The Seekers. *The chief of the Federal Bureau of Narcotics in Washington said every parent should read the book. The intelligentsia, including the educators, called it a scare book. It was published 20 years too soon.*

The Artist

He was an artist, the most unusual artist I had ever met. A lawyer by trade. He painted replicas of the great works of the French masters, and you couldn't tell them apart from the originals. He did Matisses, Monets, Lautrecs, Van Goghs, Cezannes and all the rest, and he painted any one of his masterpieces in a day. Not even Toulouse Lautrec, between slugs of brandy in the Moulin Rouge, could have put a can-can girl on canvas any faster.

I had heard about this lawyer from a client, who had just got out of a stir, as they say. He was part of a gang that would do anything to make a dishonest dollar. They were cutthroats, if I ever saw any. But a criminal lawyer, like a newspaperman, can't choose his company. It goes with the franchise. I figured if this goon could rave about a picture there must be something unusual about it. So I called and visited the lawyer's studio to take a look at his gallery. He had paintings and canvases all over the place. It looked like the back room of a museum. Lawyers come in all sizes and shapes, but he didn't look like my idea of a legal eagle. He was a little guy, and he wore a beret, French style. He had a toothbrush mustache that looked like it had been trimmed in one of those glitzy French barbershops, and sandy hair that fell all over his face. He was wearing an artist's smock. It had splotches of paint on it in all the colors of the rainbow. Some of it had stuck to his hands and face. He looked like an under-sized house painter.

He gave me an appraising look when I came in. Other than that, you would have never known his profession. His quarters were untidy, the furniture just thrown together. There were mementos of Paris all over the place. Banners, cushions, photographs of the Champs Elysées, of Notre Dame and the Arc de Triomphe, and the bridges that spanned the Seine.

I asked him if he was French or of French origin. He shook his head and said with a smile, "Not in this life."

I gave him a quick look, but he had picked up one of his Matisses and was giving it a critical look.

"What do you think of it?"

I didn't know what to say, since I wasn't familiar with Matisse. So he brought out a photograph of the original that he had worked from. I couldn't tell the difference, except I would have had to give him a shade the better of it if I had been a judge.

He was a good host. He sat me down at a table, gave me a French cigarette, which I didn't smoke, and some French toast, with French coffee, which tasted like any other coffee.

It somehow reminded me of his earlier remark.

"What did you mean, 'Not in this life'?"

"Nothing much. I just get a feeling at times of having been a French artist. As if I knew the painters I work with, and how they worked. That's how I get them down like I do."

He laughed, an embarrassed little laugh. "Of course, I don't believe in reincarnation or anything like that. It's just a feeling I have, like Jung's theory of the collective unconscious and racial memory."

I let it go at that. He was getting into something I hadn't yet resolved to my own satisfaction. Anyway I didn't have to think about it. For at that moment the room began to shake and a chandelier overhead started to sway. The table rocked, and the coffee shot out of my cup and hit the ceiling. I blinked a little and held on to my chair, which was shaking under me. I looked across the table. He was sitting up, pretty cool, L.A. cool. Without batting an eye, he reached for the coffee pot and said, "Would you like a refill?"

I was wondering where I could hide, and he was asking me about a refill. I suppose you had to be cool when you worked with the mugs he defended. Some of them I'd talked to looked like they could yank nails out of boards with their teeth and make pasta out of them. I had a coffee shake.

"What's an artist like you doing with all those gorillas?" I said when things quieted down. He shrugged his narrow shoulders. He had a nice little smile, and the name Jerry fit him like a glove.

"Look," he said, dismissing the pictures on his wall with a wave of his arm. "I have to get a grubstake or I'll never get to Paris and study my great masters in their old haunts. I want to be painting the rest of my life." He sighed. "It takes money to be an artist. I'm working on it. I've got a big case going. When it's settled . . ." His voice trailed off.

What had got a lawyer for a bunch of crooks painting like Gaugin obsessed? Nothing about him suggested the artist, except his shabby clothes and long hair. He looked a little like Van Gogh on a bad day, except he had both his ears. He needed them to listen to the stories his rumdum clients kept telling him. Whenever they dropped in, he'd make a face but he'd go off to a corner and listen. There were two or three of them. I saw the client who introduced me to Jerry only once. He was spending his time at the racetrack. His doctor told him the fresh air and sunshine were good for him. It seemed an odd place for a health cure, but I didn't argue. Not with a gun poking out of his inside pocket.

There was always a frown on Jerry's face when he finished with them.

"I wish they wouldn't bother me when I'm painting," he said, taking an hour to finish off a Cezanne he had started that morning. "They distract me."

I looked at the picture. The man was a genius. It looked just like the Cezanne in his coffee table book, a full-color replica of the French master at his best.

I looked at the names on his canvases. They were all French. Not a German or a Dutch or an Italian master among them, not to mention English or American.

"Why do you only do the French?"

He shook his head, looking solemn.

"I have wondered about that myself. I told you I felt close to the French people and everything French. And not a drop of French blood in me." His face lighted up, as though an earthshaking thought had struck him. "Maybe it's because I like Parisian food. I read somewhere that you are what you eat."

"That might make you a crêpe Suzette or a vanilla frappe."

I had seen him three or four times. And had gotten to like the little guy and what he was doing. But I still wasn't prepared for his generous offer.

"I'd like to give you a picture or two," he said one day. "I know you appreciate good art."

I had to laugh to myself, I wouldn't have known a Matisse from a Rembrandt if their names hadn't been spelled out on the canvases.

"I wouldn't feel right about it. You could sell them."

He looked at the stacks of paintings cluttering his studio. "I can't bring myself to that. It would be like selling my children."

"You might sell enough to set you up in Paris."

He stopped painting to give me a serious look.

"No, that wouldn't do. I'll make it on my law practice. As I told you, I have a big case coming up. If I win that I got it made. I won't need anything else."

He was very mysterious.

"I don't want any publicity right now. I'm trying to keep a low profile until the case blows over, and then I'll head for France." His eyes glowed like Paris at night. "To spend the rest of my days in Gay Paree."

I kept dropping around. There was something about him that intrigued me. I didn't know whether it was preoccupation with the French style or the mysterious conferences he was having with the thugs he called his clients. He told me he was trying his big case out of town. He was so secretive I thought there might be a story. But he only shrugged. When I called his maid said he'd be back in a few days.

I dropped in on him the day after he got back. He looked a little tired, but I could see he was bursting with excitement.

He gave me a quizzical look. "Do you think you could sell any of my pictures?"

"No problem," I said. "I'll take a few myself."

He shook his head. "That won't do, I want you to have the money from them."

I was astounded. "I couldn't take anything from you. It wouldn't be right. I won't even think about it."

I could see from his eyes he was preoccupied with something that had to come out. I felt sure it was what he had been keeping back, and that it had to do with the hoodlums he worked for.

He paced his studio, looking at the floor as if the answer to his problem would rise and hit him in the eyes. He turned to me with a look of dumb appeal.

"I have to tell somebody," he cried, "or I'll explode. But you can't print it. That's why I want you to have the pictures. I want you to have something. There's nobody else I can talk to."

No reporter liked stories he couldn't put in the paper. It was like a tree falling without anybody there to see it fall. It never happened. Not for a reporter.

"Please," he said. "I can't keep it to myself."

His eyes were rolling and his hand trembling in his excitement. He had been so cool I knew it must be something of an incredible nature.

"All right," I said, with an air of resignation. At least my curiosity would be appeased.

He sat down and poured coffee with a hand that shook. It must have been a shocker, considering what little effect an earthquake had on him.

He fiddled with his cup a moment, as if considering where to begin.

"As you know I had this trial up North. It was a tough case. My three clients were charged with conspiracy. I won't bother you with technicalities. The prosecution thought they had the goods on two of them. But unless they could link the three, they couldn't get a conviction. Only then would I get the fee my clients had promised me. The prosecution had claimed the crime of itself was proof of contact. Otherwise, there would have been no crime. That gave me the opening I needed.

"I agree," I told the jury. "No crime, no contact. No contact, no crime. They haven't established the contact the law requires. It's as simple as that."

He grinned. "It was so simple the jurors thought they understood it. Even though I wasn't sure I did. They took 10 minutes to deliberate, and came back with an acquittal."

He was into his second cup of coffee. His Adam's apple was bobbing. He still hadn't mentioned the specific crime his clients were charged with. I saw no reason for mystery at this point.

"What were they accused of?"

"What difference does it make? They beat it, that's enough."

He got up from the table, and began touching up his paintings with a stroke here and there. He was nervous, trying to work off his excitement. As he kept daubing away he talked to me over his shoulder.

"I wondered what they were going to pay me. They suggested we settle up at a bar around the corner from the courthouse. They owned it. After we sat down in a booth, they ordered drinks and Pug, the one with the scar down his face, handed me an envelope. As I tore it open, they looked at me with expectant smiles."

As he examined the contents a lump came to his throat. It was a large enough sum by ordinary standards but not what he had expected after months of labor. It would not give him a life in Paris. It was for $30,000, in thousand-dollar bills.

The head gorilla saw his disappointment and gave him a stony look.

"You ain't satisfied?"

"Oh, yes," said Jerry, "I just thought from what you said . . ."

The three crooks broke into gales of laughter, tears rolled down their cheeks.

"I think I'll be going," said Jerry, half-rising from the table.

The gorilla pressed one finger against Jerry's chest. "Sit down. And listen."

He pointed to the money Jerry was stuffing back into the envelope.

"Take that money, all of it. Take it to the track tomorrow. Put it on the number five horse in the sixth race. Then tell us you haven't been paid right and you'll wear your head upside down."

My attention was caught.

"Did you bet it?" There was awe in my voice.

Jerry had never been to a racetrack in his life. He had never made a bet, not even two dollars. He wanted to trim his losses, taking the money and putting it in the bank. If he stinted it might give him a year or two in his beloved Paris.

"I had no choice. They drove me to the track the next day, and marched me up to the betting window." It was marked Special Wagers. Almost in agony he handed the $30,000 to a teller whose eyes almost jumped out of their sockets. Betting a horse who had never won a race.

By this time I was more excited than Jerry. I broke in, "And the race? What happened?"

The men had been watching him with mirthless smiles. And then they began to laugh among themselves.

"I guess we fixed you," the gorilla chortled.

They walked into the clubhouse, and the ushers made a great show of taking Jerry's clients to their box. They were obviously habitués of the place. Jerry's chin dropped as he saw the odds on the tote board. His horse was 100-to-1. He knew enough about horses to know that no horse was a 100-to-1 unless he had absolutely no chance to win the race. He would be lucky to finish.

His bet changed the odds. The horse came down to a respectable 15-to-1. This meant Jerry would get almost a half-million dollars if number five did the impossible. He didn't remember the horse's name. It was just a number to him.

He was almost numb by the time he saw the horses enter the gate. It didn't get any better. As they went off, his horse stumbled and dropped back behind the leaders, running a dismal last in a field of eight. He rallied at the first turn as the other horses appeared to get into all kinds of trouble, lugging out at the turn, bumping, tangling with the rail. One even threw his jockey, just as it looked like he might break away. Old Number Five, like the turtle who had taken on the hare, came plodding along, passing one horse after another who had run into trouble.

I could contain myself no longer. I took Jerry by the sleeve and began pulling on him.

"Who won? Tell me. I'm dying."

He smiled his mysterious smile, and opened a tin box which had been sitting under the table. He put in his hand and came out with more thousand-dollar bills than I would see in a dozen lifetimes.

"Count it," he said. "Almost a half-million."

I looked at him with new respect. Not because he had won. But it wasn't every day you met a man who bet a year's pay on a horse race.

"You deserve a lot of credit putting all that money on a 100-to-1 shot."

He smiled. "I didn't have any choice. Besides, as I got to thinking about it, I decided it was a pretty good gamble."

I looked at him in surprise.

"How did you figure that? They would never have made good on it. Not those bums."

"They weren't all that bad," he said. "They did keep their word. It was one hell of a fee. It wouldn't happen like that again in a million years."

"By the way," I said, remembering he had never told me what the charges were, "who did your clients kill?"

He seemed embarrassed.

"Nothing sinister," he said. "A victimless crime." He opened the tin box, and put the money away. "Besides, I wasn't sure they were guilty."

His eyes slipped away from mine. He went back to splashing a last swatch of paint on the backside of one of Toulouse Lautrec's dancing girls.

"The charge?" I demanded. "It can't matter now that they were exonerated."

He smiled, and put his brush away.

"I'll be leaving for Paris tomorrow. So I suppose it's all right." He handed me a Matisse, a Lautrec, and a Monet. "I want you to have these. You have been a patient listener."

"And the charge?"

"Oh, that," he said. "They were charged with fixing horse races. I can't imagine why."

Bob Hope

*I*t was a benefit to raise funds for the hearing clinic operated in Los Angeles by the famed ear specialists, Drs.
William and Howard House. Comedian Bob Hope was the
master of ceremonies. I sat at the same table with one of the
fund raisers, and a young comedian who played a small
lounge in Las Vegas. There were several hundred people in
the hotel dining room, a great number of them treated by the
House brothers for hearing loss. They were older, for the most
part, distinguished and well-off. The young comedian was getting ready to perform. He was visibly nervous in this company.

Bob Hope had stopped by our table to pay his respects to the
elderly woman who had helped arrange the benefit. His eyes
traveled down the table. He saw the youthful comedian twisting his collar and biting his lips. Worried that his Las Vegas
brand of humor wouldn't go down with the conservative crowd.

Hope put his arm around the younger man's shoulders, and
said with a straight face:

"You got nothing to worry about, Kiddo. Nobody in this
crowd can hear a word you say anyway."

Kenneth Branagh

I had been reading about the Irish actor, Kenneth Branagh. He had starred in and directed the film *Henry the V* to great acclaim. At 28, I read, he had fame and fortune, a great future, and a beautiful wife with whom he shared stardom.

He was making a new film, *Dead Again*, about reincarnation, with his wife, Emma Thompson. They seemed inseparable.

I had a chance to meet him. His studio was taking still pictures on the beach in front of my house. He was quiet and introspective, shorter than I would have thought from his stirring performance in *Henry the V*. He had been reading *Soulmates*, my book with a reincarnation theme. We chatted for a few moments.

"You are a lucky man," I said. "Twenty-eight and look where you are."

"Thirty," he said.

"You have such a talented beautiful wife."

"We're getting divorced."

He stood up and walked away.

I felt a perfect fool.

Glamour

I read where she was voted the world's most glamorous woman. And here I was sitting next to her at a dinner party given by Hollywood producer Joe Levine. She was truly a beautiful woman, unspoiled, down-to-earth, friendly, with a lively curiosity about everybody at the table.

She looked at the slim blonde model sitting on the other side of her. "You're so svelte. I envy you. I'm sure you have no trouble keeping thin for the elegant pictures you do for *Vogue* and the other fashion magazines."

The blonde lifted her eyebrows. "I would much rather be you," she said, "world-famous, the most adorable figure on the screen. And sexy. Who ever heard of a sexy fashion model? We're all bones."

Sophia Loren laughed. "Hardly," she said. She looked at the other girl's plate. She had barely picked at her food.

"I can't control myself. I'm ravenous at the sight of food. I can't help it. If I let myself go I'd weigh 200 pounds."

"Why is that, Sophia?" I asked.

She turned away from the blonde.

"Rome. The war was on. There was no food. I was six years old. I woke up hungry and went to bed hungry. If it hadn't been for the garbage pails I would have starved to death."

She looked down the table at the people enjoying their desserts. Her eyes dropped to her own empty plate. "I've had a full dinner and I'm still hungry. I'm always hungry. The brain may forget but the body remembers." She sighed. "The garbage pails won't go away."

Not even for the world's most glamorous woman.

A Malibu Star

Hollywood stars were a dime a dozen in Malibu. Who could get excited about Paul Newman pushing a cart around the supermarket, or Charles Bronson sitting in a dark corner of a restaurant, glowering. As for Ryan O'Neal, is he the guy that's living with Farrah Fawcett? Or is it Olivia Newton-John, or Linda Ronstadt? It's hard to get all those names straight, particularly when, like Tom Cruise or Dustin Hoffman, they keep moving in and out. Like Shirley MacLaine, who's always going somewhere.

I saw George C. Scott squinting to read the fine print on a can of vegetables, and wondered what had happened to General Patton. George is still my favorite, next to Mel Gibson who plays Mad Max like there's no tomorrow. When there's a lot of celebrities, I guess there's no celebrities. Except for one. And I had the distinction to live next door to him. And when I say next door, I mean inches apart, on the beach.

He was sort of a celebrity's celebrity, standing apart without any effort. He'd nod and speak to me once in a while. And I'd feel inflated all over. I would have liked to have asked how it went on the road, and did it look as easy as he made it look.

But I could tell he didn't like long conversations. "Hello, how are you?" or a big fat "Hi." That's as good as it got. I would have liked his autograph for the kids, but I was afraid he might move away or ask me if I was selling my house.

He was tall and sinewy, with an athlete's build, and an actor's profile. He moved with grace and precision. When you saw him. That wasn't always possible. There were so many people standing on their toes to look into his windows that he put blinds on the rails that enclosed his deck. It wasn't that he didn't like people. He liked his privacy more. And, of course, you'd know that when he married, it wouldn't be some actress or other, but the beautiful non-actress daughter of a famous actor. Richard Widmark's pride and joy.

Privacy was his fetish. I guess it was because he couldn't go anywhere without people wanting to touch him, or have a word or two. One day he looked down the beach and saw three people at a distance. "It's getting crowded," he said. "I think I'll be moving on."

He did move on, but not before he pitched the greatest game anybody ever pitched. Not like any of the no-hitters he pitched, or where he kept striking out the other side inning after inning. But in the World Series, in a game that everybody knew was to be his last. Because at the age of 31 or so, all those strikes he threw did something to an arm that looked like it would go on forever. He was pitching for his beloved Dodgers, the only team he ever pitched for, against the hated Yankees. He had gone into the ninth inning, wincing with every throw, sustained by raw nerve and pride, not yielding a run. The huge crowd was cheering him on, even the rival gang, loving him, knowing they were watching the swan song of an American legend. Empathizing with every pitch he hurled, hoping he would bring it off. Only one more inning. Neither side had scored. Three more batters and he would have his shutout. A crowning achievement even if he was in agony with every pitch.

A fly ball went out to center field. The crowd breathed easier. An easy out. But, no, the fielder, the usually adroit Willie Davis, faltered in the sun and the ball popped out of his glove. The crowd groaned. There was a man on first. The next batter. Another fly ball to center field. An easy out. Again the ball went to the center fielder. Again a ball lost in the sun. Two men on base. He was struggling. But still calm and composed, no vestige of distress or frustration on his hawk-like face.

The crowd was sizzling now. The inning should have been nearly over. The pitch came like a fireball toward home plate. The batter swung and the ball sailed out to center field. Willie Davis raced to get under it, and again the sun struck him in such a way that he lost the ball. Two runs came in. Sandy Koufax walked off the mound, not finishing the last game of baseball he would ever play.

The huge crowd stood up and gave him an ovation the likes of which they had never given a winner. He trudged off to the showers, outscored but not defeated. His shoulders were still thrown back, but the fatigue lines were etched on his lean face and his arm felt like it was about to drop off.

The drama did not end there. For the quiet-spoken Sandy Koufax was not just the greatest of pitchers. But of the stuff that heroes are made.

The reporters flooded into the locker room after the game was lost. He was sitting in front of his locker, too tired to move. Too tired to even look up. When the reporters descended on him.

"How do you feel about Willie Davis losing all those fly balls and costing you the last triumph of your career?"

Sandy looked up, peering into the reporter's eyes.

"All I know," he said, "is that he caught a lot of fly balls for me all through the season."

The General

There was a homecoming for the general at the academy where he had trained for the supreme command of the armies of the Western world. It was to be a quiet affair, sort of family. He had requested no interviews, looking to relax with old classmates and say a few words to the thin gray line that would follow him.

I was not to interview the general, just spend the day with him, walking around the campus where he had walked so many years before. I could make idle conversation, if he seemed agreeable. But my only reason for being there was to feel him out on the presidency. I was given one question to ask, and only one. Off the record. And that question, not to be misunderstood:

"Would you consider being a candidate for the presidency of the United States?"

It was all arranged by the Old Man. The man that owned our paper. Nobody else could have managed. He had been in the military himself, and prided himself on his knowledge of tactics.

I didn't look at my mission as being of transcending importance, though I did like the idea of visiting with a man who held the fate of the Western world in his hands through some uneasy years. He was one of the few public figures who liked newspapermen. Maybe because he didn't stand on ceremony with them. He was the small-town boy whose head never got bigger than his job.

I couldn't help liking him. He grabbed my hand and gave me his famous ear-to-ear grin. He was dripping with charm. He was so easygoing it reminded me of the story about his helping an overburdened subaltern with his bags while the field marshals and command generals were gathering for the last push of the war.

He blushed like a young lieutenant with his pants on wrong when I mentioned the story.

"He's a fine officer," he said of the subaltern. That was all he would say. But it did get him talking about the enemy counter-offensive in the Ardennes forest that had the Allied forces reeling on their heels in the final fighting.

"It was touch and go. They broke our lines and disrupted our communications. We were thoroughly confused."

I looked at him in surprise. I had never read anything like that.

"Then how did we beat them?"

He laughed, that contagious laugh everybody knew so well.

"We hit them with every plane we had. Until they were more confused than we were."

We had been striding along at a brisk pace, his officer entourage keeping a discreet distance. I had nothing more except what I had been sent to say. He seemed in such a good mood I chose this moment for my question.

"General, would you consider being president of the United States?"

He looked up with a start, then came to a stop. His eyes held me in a steely grip. The smile had left his face.

"You must be kidding."

"No," I said, "this is the well-considered question of a patriot who feels you are the man the nation needs in the White House."

He had no more to say.

We resumed walking as though nothing had been said.

I made another attempt. He shook his head. "I'm complimented, but I have no more to say on the subject. We already have a commander in chief and he sits in Washington."

As we moved on so did his retinue. I saw a few curious looks, but the aides kept their distance. Not so two young noncommissioned officers, a sergeant and corporal, who had been standing off a little ways, waiting to beard the general. They approached in a hesitant fashion, each with a slip of paper in his hand. The general paused and gave them a smile. I stood to one side. They were so nervous their hands shook. I hardly blamed them. They were confronting the most famous soldier in the world. Their commander in chief.

They saluted, and the general saluted. The sergeant spoke for the pair. "General," he said, gulping, "would you be kind enough to autograph these slips of paper for us? We would greatly appreciate it."

The general held out his hand, and scanned the slips, turning each one of them over. They were blank. The sergeant proffered a pen for the general's signature.

Their general ignored the pen and scowled.

His lips twitched, and the cords in his neck bulged. He kept looking at the slips as if he couldn't believe what he saw.

He had been so obliging I had expected him to dash off his signature with a smile and give the noncoms a treat they would remember the rest of their lives.

Instead, stiffly, he handed the slips back, unsigned. "You men should know better," he said in a rasping voice. "I could have you court-martialed for giving a blank chit to a superior officer for his signature."

The two men seemed to shrink into the ground.

He paused for a moment, then waved them off. "Consider yourselves lucky you're not held for discipline."

They slunk off like whipped dogs.

I was stunned by this turn of events. I watched them draw off, sympathizing with them every step of the way. My surprise must have been apparent, for the general turned to me and said:

"You didn't like that, did you?"

I hesitated.

"You were their hero, General."

The general gave me another look. "You know that was a serious offense. Anybody could put a command order over that signature, and move half-a-dozen divisions into battle."

"I'm sure you're right, General," I said without enthusiasm, not daring to ask who these divisions would do battle with.

He turned again, saw that his entourage was well out of range, and then spotted the two noncoms retreating slowly with their heads down.

"Men," he called out in a voice that could have cleared a canyon. "Men, come back." He motioned at the same time, so there would be no doubt what he meant.

Just as they had slunk off, they now came sidling back. As they drew closer, I could see the fear in their faces.

"Come here, men," he said in a resolute voice. "On the double."

They broke into a feeble trot.

They stopped a few feet from the general, at attention.

"Let me see those slips of paper again."

They fumbled in their pockets and came up with the blank slips with trembling hands.

His face was solemn. He pointed to a building on the campus grounds. "I am staying at that hotel," he said. "Leave your pieces of paper with the desk. Tell them to see they are delivered to my quarters after you put your names on them." He smiled. "Make sure they are not blank."

He paused.

"I will sign them, and leave them at the desk in your name."

He saluted them smartly.

I had never seen two faces undergo such a transition so quickly. They stood stiff and erect, and saluted as if they were an elite corps.

"Thank you, sir, thank you," they cried in unison, as he dismissed them with a friendly wave of his hand.

We watched them move off. They appeared to be floating on air.

He looked at me with a grin.

"Satisfied?"

I took a deep breath. What he had done meant more than he realized. For he had been my idol as well.

"I am sure, General, that you will one day be president of the United States."

And he was. For eight friendly years.

The Irreversible Crime

The judge was the greatest criminal lawyer to ever cast a spell over a jury. He had defended a hundred killers without losing a case. Invading the Deep South he got off the seven Scottsboro boys facing execution for allegedly raping a white woman, then a capital crime. And stood up to a hostile mob with a smile.

He did a complete turnabout on the bench, advocating capital punishment, to the horror of the liberals who felt he had betrayed them.

I wondered about this change of heart.

"There's no mystery about it," he said as we lunched in his chambers. "It was my job as a lawyer to defend the people who came to me for help. Now it's my job as a judge to protect society from criminals I had once sworn to defend."

It seemed rather cynical to me.

He shrugged, reading my mind. "Capital punishment is a deterrent. The only consideration that will stop a killer. That he may pay in kind. An eye for an eye, and a tooth for a tooth."

"How about the accused convicted, executed, then found to be innocent when new evidence turns up. The irreversible crime. By the state."

He grunted. "I can't agree, despite all the fuss the do-good-ers and bleeding hearts make of it."

I had picked up an article, where the still grieving widow of Bruno Richard Hauptmann, executed in the Lindbergh baby kidnaping, was renewing her fight to establish her dead husband's innocence.

"How about the Lindbergh case? Why would the wife be knocking herself out after all these years?"

He looked up from his plate in disgust. "Nonsense, the man was as guilty as hell."

"Why did he die protesting his innocence? It served no purpose."

"For his wife and two small children—and posterity."

I handed him the article. The case had been hazy in my mind. Before my time as a reporter. A cause célèbre because the father, Charles Lindbergh, the Lone Eagle, was a nation's hero. The persevering widow appeared to have a telling point or two, making a case for a husband who could no longer speak for himself.

Hauptmann was the only person charged in the crime. No accomplices were named. And yet it seemed improbable that one man could have carried out the kidnaping, particularly a foreigner unfamiliar with the terrain of the Lindbergh home in a remote area of New Jersey.

How could he have managed it alone? Taking the child from the second-floor bedroom of a secluded home well-staffed with servants. How did he know which bedroom to go to? Leaning a ladder against the house at the right spot, then going up and down the ladder, carrying the baby on his return, without waking anybody in the household. Without an outcry from the child. The child apparently dropped and killed. I wondered, too, about his counsel.

"They say his lawyer didn't do as well as he could have."

"He did as well as anybody could, with all the public senti-ment running against him."

"Did you know him?"

He smiled. "I recommended him. After I turned down the case."

I looked at him in disbelief.

"You turned down the case? The Crime of the Century?"

It didn't seem like him. Not after what he said about defending people. He thrived on attention as a lawyer. Every word he uttered in that tiny New Jersey courtroom would have flashed across the world.

"I had good and sufficient reason," he said, settling back in his chair, and staring off into space for a few moments. "I haven't told any of this before." He frowned. "But perhaps I should for the record."

He sighed and nodded a few times, as he had a way of doing when he was deep in thought. His voice, usually reso-nant, was so soft I had to lean forward to hear him clearly.

"I had mixed feelings about the case. It had become an international issue. Hauptmann's cause was being champi-oned by Hitler and the Nazis at the time Jews were being persecuted in Germany. I was a Jew. I defended scores of people accused of murder, but never a child kidnaper.

"All this weighed heavily on my mind when the newspaper tycoon, William Randolph Hearst, asked me to take the case. Like so many, he thought Hauptmann innocent. And that he was being railroaded to the chair. A friendless alien in a hos-tile land, accused, in effect, of a heinous crime against the man an adoring nation called Lucky Lindy, the first man to fly the Atlantic.

"Mr. Hearst was insistent, so sure of Hauptmann's inno-cence that he cast a doubt in my mind. I agreed to visit Hauptmann in the New Jersey prison cell where he was awaiting trial, and judge for myself."

There were no strictures on his visit. He was allowed whatever time he needed. He made no fixed appointment. So the meeting would have some element of surprise.

As he entered the cell, Hauptmann was sitting on the edge of his cot. His head was bowed. As he looked up slowly, the judge saw a man with guarded eyes in a gaunt face. He had the look of a hunted animal. But for only a moment.

"He gave me a shrewd appraising look. It was a peasant's face, rough-hewn, with sharp features, and a peasant's superstitions. He was 35 or so, with a prison pallor. He seemed composed.

"I introduced myself. He nodded, reaching out to shake my hand. His hand felt cold and clammy, unpleasant to the touch. This was not unusual with men at death's door.

"I looked around the tiny cell. It was bare of anything with which he could have harmed himself. Not even a bedsheet which he could have torn into strips and hanged himself. There were no overhead fixtures. I had a feeling the precautions were unnecessary. This was a man who wanted to live.

"There were two pictures on the wall. They were framed photographs. One of a pleasant-looking blonde woman about his own age. The other of two golden-haired children, with bright handsome faces.

"He saw my questioning look. He nodded at the woman's picture. There was a look of pride in his eye. 'My wife,' he said. He spoke in the heavy guttural voice of a middle European with no schooling in the English language. Little different from others of his countrymen in the same station in life. There was nothing distinctive about his appearance or manner.

"However, all this changed when he looked at the picture of his children. 'Mein Liebchen,' he whispered. His face grew radiant, and his eyes glowed with a holy light. 'Mein

Liebchen,' he repeated, adding in his clumsy English, 'My dear own loved ones.'

"He sighed and there were tears in his eyes. 'I love them more than life itself.'

"I sat down on the cot, facing him. I explained that everything that transpired between us was confidential. He nodded, comprehending, saying he had nothing to hide.

"I had noticed a prison Bible on the ledge of a barred window above his cot."

"'Are you a Christian?'"

"'Oh, yes.'

"'You believe then in God?'

"'Oh, yes, yes.' He was profuse in his acknowledgment.

"I explained that as a lawyer it made no difference to me whether he was guilty or innocent, that in any event I was sworn to defend an accused person, who was presumed innocent until proven guilty.

"He puzzled over this for a moment. 'You would help me if I was guilty?' He looked at me in disbelief.

"'If everything else was in order, that would not affect my decision. I have defended more than a hundred killers in my time and I never lost one to the chair.'

"His eyes widened, and he looked at me as if I was some sort of wizard or monster, which, he was not quite sure. He looked solemn.

"'I am not a killer,' he said. 'I commit no crime. I do not kill or kidnap that little child.'

"'Good,' I said, reaching for the Bible. 'Then you will swear your innocence on this Bible?'

"He nodded several times. 'Ja, ja, ja.'

"I placed the Bible in his lap, and put his hand on it. He looked up at me with wondering eyes.

"'Repeat after me,' I said.

"'I do hereby swear on my life that I had nothing to do with the death or kidnaping of that innocent child.'"

The Judge allowed himself a thin smile. "I knew he would swear to this. I was ready for the next oath. I picked up the photograph of his wife. I repeated the procedure. He had no trouble with this, either. His eyes were the picture of wide-eyed innocence as he repeated the oath after me. Looking at me with dumb appeal, he cried out in an agonized voice, 'I have my own dear Liebchen. How could I harm a hair of an innocent child?'

"I had seen men protest their innocence before, with such vehemence that I was sure they had convinced themselves of their innocence. It was not that unusual, for the mind often believes what it wants to believe, when the truth is too unpleasant to be faced.

"I was not finished. I took the picture of his children, and handed it to him. They were lovely children, and their eyes looked out guilelessly from the gold-edged picture frame. His eyes had a soulful look as he considered the features so dear to him.

"'Now listen closely,' I said, 'and repeat after me, word for word, what I say.' He gulped a little and his Adam's apple bobbed, but his expression did not change. I made my voice suit the occasion. It became fuller, with greater resonance. It was the voice of a preacher breathing fire and brimstone at the sinners in his flock."

His hand was on the picture as the Judge exclaimed in a voice of doom:

"'May my children suffer a horrible and violent death, may they rot in purgatory and be eternally damned if I kidnaped or killed that innocent child.'"

The judge had been watching the prisoner, looking for some sign of hesitation. He saw more than he had anticipated. The prisoner began to shake. He clutched the picture to his chest.

Beads of perspiration stood out on his forehead and trickled down into his eyes. He opened his mouth, but no words escaped, only a throaty rattle that turned into a gasp and a sob. He threw his head up and made a new effort to speak. No words issued from his lips, only the croaking of a broken man.

He felt only pity for this shell of a man. Forgotten for the moment was the heinousness of the crime, and the reason for his visit. He was looking at a man convicted by his own conscience.

He touched the prisoner's shoulder. "Listen to me carefully," he said. "I cannot take your case, not because you may be guilty. I make no judgment of this. But because you were not open with me. I cannot represent a client I cannot trust. I cannot trust a client who is not truthful with me."

The prisoner did not lift his head. It was still bowed when a guard came, and the cell door closed after the Judge.

The story had taken something out of the Judge. The lines in his face seemed deeper, the wrinkles in his forehead more pronounced. He had relived that day as if it were yesterday. It had been a harrowing experience. He was not the man of stone his critics made him.

"I have relived that trial a thousand times, and I was never there."

He looked up at the ceiling. His eyes seemed to fall away into time. His face cleared, and the years slipped away. His eyes glowed, all else forgotten but the defense he had contrived in his mind. He was in the courtroom where another lawyer had stood in his stead years before. He was standing before the judge and the jury with the eyes of the world on him. The fatigue lines left his face. He looked 20 years younger, as he would have looked in court.

"The prosecution had little but circumstantial evidence. There was no confession, no witnesses. I would have disposed of the ladder used to reach the baby's room, the ransom money, the best of the circumstantial evidence, by planting a reasonable doubt in the minds of the jurors. He lived in a rooming-house with many transients. Anybody could have planted the money on him, or put the ladder in his garage, for any variety of reasons. None of this convicted him. There was only one piece of direct evidence in the case. And that took him to the chair. It was the testimony of the hero father, swearing from the stand that the prisoner's voice was the voice of the man he had passed the ransom money to on that dark and memorable night. Without knowing his child was already dead. It was a moment, Lindbergh swore, he would never forget. Nor could he forget or mistake that voice. It was etched indelibly on his brain, along with the face of his dead child.

"The jury could not help but be swayed by the father's quiet conviction. They condemned the accused. And he was executed."

I was baffled. He said he had taken himself out of the case because the prisoner wasn't open. But how could he trust any of the thugs and murderers who had lied their way into his care? There had to be more.

"Were you afraid of losing your first case?"

"That wasn't what I was afraid of. I was afraid I would win it."

The dark, craggy face lit up. He was in a crowded courtroom, once more a counselor-at-law, pleading for a man's life as only he could.

"I would have made a recording of my client's voice, and of five or six voices with heavy accents similar to his. All recording the few words spoken that night in the dark. The voices would have been those of a professional actor, expert at ethnic imitations. He would have mastered every inflection and peculiarity of Hauptmann's speech. By the time he was done, not even the accused's wife could have told the two voices apart. I would have blindfolded the child's father, a defense counsel's prerogative with a man's life at stake, to simulate the darkness. As he sat blindfolded on the stand, I would have played the six records, including that of my client's. I would have asked him to pick out the voice of the accused. He would have been thoroughly confused. The odds were against him. One mistake and his testimony was demolished."

He stared off into space as if visualizing the jurors filing back into the courtroom with their verdict.

"The jury would have had no choice, regardless of their sympathies. And he would have beaten the chair. Another monster would have been released into the world. And that would have been the irreversible crime."

Denson

"Let's lunch someplace quiet," said John Denson. "Someplace we can talk about the magazine."

I had no idea what *Newsweek's* chief editor could get out of a subordinate who had been on the magazine for only two or three months. And was still trying to figure out what he was doing there. He saw my hesitation.

"We're newspapermen," he said. "The rest of these guys are *Time* and *Life*rs. We understand each other."

We wound up at Toots Shor's. A habitat of the sports world. Everybody went there. Joe DiMaggio, Ted Williams, Namath, Willie Shoemaker. And the people who went there to look at them.

We hadn't settled in at our table before we had a visitor. Jimmy Cannon, the Hearst newspapers' star sportwriter, an articulate Irish Catholic and a voluble admirer of the Irish boxers: Gene Tunney, Jimmy McLarnin, Corbett and the great John L.

"Can I sit with you guys?" Jimmy said, stretching his legs under the table.

Denson nodded. "Just don't bust our eardrums."

Jimmy had just come back from Muhammed Ali's training camp and was bursting with stories about the heavyweight champ.

"Want to hear a hot one?" he said.

John picked at his teeth and looked around for a waiter. He always looked for a waiter when somebody was about to tell a story.

"Yeah, go on," he said. "We don't have much time. We got a magazine to put out."

That made no impression on Jimmy. He'd known Denson a long time.

"Anyway, guess what Muhammed Ali is doing?" He shook his craggy Irish face. "He's sending Stephen Fetchit to Israel. You know, the black comedian who pokes around like molasses going up a hill in January."

Denson came to life for a moment. "To Israel? Why the hell would he be doing that?"

Jimmy's eyes glowed like a priest about to say his first novena.

"You won't believe it. But I got it from the horse's mouth.

"Ali's got a bee in his bonnet. It's crazy. Beats anything I've ever heard."

Denson looked mildly interested.

"I thought Ali did all his talking in public."

Jimmy shook his head. "This is sub rosa. You know, heavy stuff."

"So he told you?"

"Not for the paper. Nobody would believe it anyway."

He sat back and rolled his eyes.

"Ali, believe it or not, thinks Jesus Christ was a black man. That's why he's sending Stephen Fetchit to the Holy Land. To mosey around the place. Check the records. Maybe look at the Dead Sea Scrolls. Walk the 14 Stations of the Cross."

He looked around like he'd just dropped a bomb in the middle of a parade.

Denson was still picking his teeth, and scanning a menu he'd scanned a thousand times.

Jimmy turned to me. "What do you say to that? I think the guy's taken one punch too many."

I caught a wink from Denson and nodded. "I can see why you're upset, Jimmy. Everybody knows Jesus was an Irish Catholic."

Jimmy stood up and left. "I'll see you guys later."

"Now," said Denson, "we can talk about the magazine."

More Denson

"Well, kid," John Denson said, "you've been here six months. That makes you kind of permanent. You know, pension rights, medical, all the perks. Not," he laughed, "that you'll be around long enough to get any of these things."

I laughed with him. I knew better than he how right he was. After working with newspapers for 20 years, writing pretty much how I pleased, I had never been able to get into the swing of being a group writer for a weekly news magazine. By the time three editors had told me three different ways to write some insignificant story, I was ready to pack my bag and head for the woods. Yet I kept hoping lightning would strike one day and I could handle an ordinary story in the ordinary way.

I thought of humorist Jim Thurber going off to write a news story about a missing girl in the Bronx, and coming back with a romantic tale about a fairy princess who had been kidnaped by a wicked dragon. I wasn't as creative as Thurber and I needed a job more than he did. And so I kept trying.

Anyway, Denson was taking me to lunch to commemorate

224

the occasion of my transition. I enjoyed these lunches. We didn't say much. He always ordered the same thing. Melted cheese, laced with Worcestershire sauce. He didn't seem to enjoy it but he managed to put it away.

"Well," he said across the table, "I guess after six months you've got a few suggestions on how we can improve the magazine." He yawned. "Everybody does."

"I haven't given it much thought, John. I'm having my own problems."

"You must have some suggestions. Or observations."

I reflected. "As a matter of fact you're right. I do have one suggestion."

His face brightened, and he became immediately attentive. The luncheon wouldn't be a complete dud after all.

"Let's hear it," he said.

"You know how we triple space, writing our stories? And the various editors make corrections and additions between the lines?"

"Of course I know. Who do you think I am, the bat boy?"

"Well, I think we should quadruple space."

"What good would that do?"

I paused. "It would give another jackass a chance to add to the confusion."

He wiped his lips with a napkin and waved for the check.

"I should have known better," he said. "You newspaper guys are all the same. No respect."

He was right. I wasn't around long enough to enjoy any of the perks. It was nobody's fault but mine. I didn't know how to read between the lines.

The Sheraton File

"How," I asked the cofounder and chairman of the Sheraton hotels, "did you get your start?"

Robert Moore's face broke into a smile, reminding me of his daughter, Marcia, the mercurial teacher who had brought me to Concord to write a book on yoga.

He took a modest sip of his drink.

"It all began when Ernie Henderson and I got out of Harvard. We didn't have any money. But we had energy and imagination. We borrowed some money and bought a big lot of suits for a dollar apiece. We didn't see how we could go wrong. We put together some strong mail-order ads, with a money-back guarantee.

"The money began pouring in. We kept sending out the suits as fast as the orders came in. And then the suits started coming back. A few at first, then a regular torrent. We looked at each other and shook our heads. It was a nightmare. We not only had to pay out the refunds, but the extra mailing charges. And then, to our consternation, we learned the suits were being sent back because they shrank in the rain. There was nothing we could do about the rain. It seemed hopeless.

"And then we noticed a peculiar thing. Everybody had sent the suits back, but one man. And he kept reordering. He was somewhere in the Middle West.

"Ernie decided it might be a good idea if he went out there and found out why this man kept buying the suits."

He took another taste of his drink. By this time I was sitting on the edge of my seat.

"And so what did he find?"

He permitted his patrician features to dissolve into a smile.

"Ernie came back in a few days. He walked into our little office with a straight face as though nothing had changed.

"'You know what, Bob,'" he said. "'The mystery's solved. The suits we sent this man didn't shrink.'"

"How could that be, Ernie? They all came out of the same batch."

"'Yeah, but this man happens to be an undertaker.'"

I laughed along with Mr. Moore. He was so dignified. I couldn't think of him without some designation of respect.

"We resumed our mail-order operation. With a new focus. We checked the names and addresses of funeral parlors throughout the country. And let them know of our low-price suits. In no time we sold them all. With the money we bought our first hotel."

I had one question.

"Did you guarantee these suits against shrinking?"

He smiled. "It wasn't necessary."

Don't Shake
My Tree

"If you don't like my peaches, don't shake my tree." That's all Mae West had to say, and it broke up audiences. Her movies *Klondike Annie* and *She Done Him Wrong* saved Paramount Pictures during the Depression. She took her pay in Paramount stock when the studio didn't have the cash. It made her the richest woman in Hollywood.

In private she was anything but what she appeared on the stage or screen. She was contemplative with a spiritual side closely linked to the metaphysical. I had come to talk movies and found myself in a discussion of the subconscious mind and the power to see into the future.

"Something must have turned you around," I said.

"Yes," she said gravely, "that something changed my life."

She was playing Chicago at the time. "Somebody told me about this remarkable man who predicted the future. Being on the skeptical side I had to see for myself. His act was playing in a hall up the street. That's how I looked at it."

It was the fall of 1941. The psychic made a few predictions that were less than earth-shaking. And then, as though predicting the weather, he said that Pearl Harbor would be bombed by Japan on December 7, that same year.

She could see people were smiling. Some walked out. She was impressed. "He had gone out on a limb. There was no way he could waffle out of it. I felt he had to know something."

He was the Reverend Jack Kelly, a spiritualist minister from Buffalo. She talked to him after the meeting. He didn't equivocate. "We will be in for a long war."

She wasn't surprised when the attack came. From that day he became her adviser. He had reaffirmed her faith. "He could only have done what he did with God's help."

Whatever the problem she'd turn to Kelly, feeling he'd have a solution. When the police called at her Hollywood home, looking for a murder suspect taken in by her sister Beverly, and now at large, Mae asked if she could make one call before they hauled her sister off to police headquarters for questioning.

"The two detectives were watching like hawks when I put through a call to Jack in Buffalo." She smiled, thinking about it. "I didn't have to say a word. That was the wonderful thing about Jack. Here he was 3,000 miles away. And he instantly knew why I'd called. He said right off, 'The man the police want has been captured in San Diego. There's nothing to worry about. Tell the detectives what I've just told you.'"

Even with all that he had done, she was still amazed. She could see the detectives eyeing her suspiciously.

"The man's been picked up in San Diego," she said.

"And you got that from a telephone call to Buffalo?"

The older of the two detectives looked at Mae as though she was mad and took Beverly by the arm.

"What harm will it do," said Mae, "to call police headquarters?"

The detective looked at her and shrugged. He had seen all her movies. She was like an old friend to him.

"Okay." He picked up the phone.

She saw him scowl and his lips tighten. Her heart sank. Could it be that Jack Kelly was wrong? He'd never been wrong before.

He was about to put down the phone when a strange look came over his face. "You mean it's coming in now over tele-type from San Diego?" He shuddered. "I can't believe it."

He rang off and looked at his partner. Then turned to Mae. "What did you say this guy's name was?"

"Jack Kelly. He lives in Buffalo like I said."

She laughed and put on one of the impersonations that made her famous. "When you get a tough one," she said with a tilt of her eyebrows, "why don't you boys come up and see me sometime? I'll call Buffalo."

More Mae West

"Can you be at my place at eight to watch a film on the Hunzas?"

"What," I said, "are the Hunzas?"

"They're people in Tibet, or some place like that. They live to be 100 and 150. The woman who took the film asked me to be sure and invite you. She's a yogi. Do you know what that is?"

"Oh, yes, she's a yoga teacher for the stars."

"Good, we'll see you tonight."

The film was ready to be shown when I arrived. There were only a handful of us. The yoga teacher who had filmed the movie, a friend of hers, Mae West, myself, and Mae's friend, Paul Novak. I took the empty chair next to Mae. The lights were dimmed, and the production came on. You could have heard the drop of a pin. To live to be a 100 or a 150, still breathing, healthy, and earning your own keep. Better, much better, than Social Security and Medicare and the kids wondering what to do with you.

The film got off to an action start. A woman in a drab skirt and blouse, with a gaunt face, was weaving cloth on an old loom that looked like it had done service on Noah's Ark. In the background I saw a man with a glassy look milling flour from a grain that was either wheat or corn. There were other people moving about with spades and hoes doing a bit of farming. It was all very healthy but on the bleak side.

Strangely, all seemed to have a similar cast of features, produced, I decided, by a similarity of expression. It was as if they were all preoccupied with the same thought at the same time. Nobody smiled, and, God forbid a laugh as they applied themselves to their tasks.

Though hovering around the century mark, their faces were unlined, though a few had grizzled brows and a cheerless way of moving about. Some of the faces were like masks I had seen of the ancient dead.

I darted a look at Mae. She was approaching 80 and still vital, still enjoying a joke and male companionship. Still taking care of business and looking forward to new projects.

There was the hint of a smile on her face. She turned her head around, then whispered in my ear.

"Do you think it's got anything to do with age?" she grinned. "It must just seem like 100 years."

Shirley MacLaine

Shirley MacLaine had a look of concern on her elfish face.

"My intellectual friends tell me that if I publish my book *Out on a Limb*, it will ruin my career."

"On the contrary," I said, "it will increase your popularity, giving you a wider audience, and a new importance to people who thought of you only as an actress."

She looked at me rather doubtfully.

"You are the intellectual," I said, "for you are ready to explore unknown and uncharted frontiers of the mind."

Her friends, I was sure, were well-intentioned, thinking that a book on reincarnation, and her belief in it, would expose her to ridicule and damage her credibility. They were on different wave lengths.

"Your integrity as a performer will lend credence to what you have written. You will find people relating to you in a personal way that will reflect favorably on your career."

"Why do you say that?"

"Recent polls show that 25 percent of adult America professes a belief in a continuous life. Another 25 percent will probably come out of the closet and acknowledge their interest with the courage you have given them through your stand for what you believe."

She seemed unconvinced.

"How can I prove reincarnation scientifically?"

I smiled. "If Sir Oliver Lodge, a Nobel Prize winner in science, couldn't do it with a book he wrote, I don't see how anyone else can."

I understood her quandary. I had been confronted with a similar problem of credibility when I began writing about the metaphysical.

"You could look at it pragmatically," I said.

She sat, waiting. Like myself, she was a Taurus and a hard sell.

"You could describe the experiences of people like General Patton, Mark Twain and Benjamin Franklin. All wrote about their experiences. Franklin said that like an old book he expected to be back with a new cover. Mark Twain dreamed of an old love who kept coming back at different times and places. And Patton, a no-nonsense soldier, remembered himself as a Roman general, describing ancient battlefields in France and Italy and going over them in this life."

Shirley was a pragmatist.

"Where," she said, "is this information?"

I mentioned a book I had written called *Yoga, Youth and Reincarnation*. She was welcome to it.

I spoke, too, about sweethearts falling in love at first sight, remembering incidents from the past which may have triggered their love in some subconscious way when Shirley said with Taurean directness, "How about you taking a stand on reincarnation?"

I had a feeling I could be more effective reporting what I had found in a detached way.

"When," she repeated, "are you coming out of the closet?"

I laughed. "That's your perception."

Out on a Limb was an immediate bestseller. It enhanced Shirley's career. She won her first Oscar for best actress in *Terms of Endearment*. Everything had come together for a woman with the courage to be a majority of one.

I never got to know what her intellectual friends had to say. I guess they never came out of their closets.

More Shirley

I was having lunch in her New York apartment with Grace Bechtold, the senior editor of Bantam Books, which was publishing Shirley MacLaine's book.

"Have you seen Shirley's manuscript?" I asked.

She frowned. "Yes, we were disappointed at the way it came out. The writing was not what we had hoped for."

"I think it will be successful," I said. "Shirley believes in herself and she has the energy to go to bat for what she believes in."

"I hope you're right," she said, dismissing the subject and going on to make a few suggestions about my own manuscript.

A few months later I was back in New York, again lunching with my favorite editor at her apartment. Shirley's *Out on a Limb* was in all the bookstore windows. One of the most talked-of books of the day. I watched her on network television. She disarmed her critics with her nimble wit and gift for repartee. She had the studio audiences with her as she turned the tables on the nitpickers.

I didn't wonder why her book was a bestseller.

"Have you noticed," I said slyly, "how well *Out on a Limb* is doing?"

"Oh, yes," said Grace with a professional nod, "it's a first-rate book."

"When," I said, with a suicidal inclination, "did you change your mind?"

She gave me a sharp glance.

"I went through it again when advance copies were made available."

"And?"

"I saw a number of things in it I'd overlooked before."

I smiled. We were friends. "I'm sure you did. And I know what they are."

She gave me a dark look.

"Don't dare say what you're thinking. Or I'll throw you out."

I had an idea we were thinking the same thing.

The Bird Woman

She took me out to the deck overlooking the pounding surf. Even in the bright sunlight, her face appeared to be without a flaw. She had the look of a goddess. Her eyes were a quiet blue, set off by a noble brow. Her flaxen hair came down in tumbling waves to her shoulders. She moved with the grace and ease of a cat.

She had a way with birds, I was told.

As we looked down the beach, I saw no sign of any birds, not even sea gulls, which were usually seen everywhere near the ocean. But as she raised her hand, they seemed to come out of nowhere. She had crumbled a loaf of bread into small pieces. She now offered them to the birds.

As she fed them the birds would fly by in formation, one or two breaking the pattern by dropping down and roosting on her arm or head. The others would scold in their squeaky way and try to displace their companions. She would smile and hand each of them a morsel of bread. Instead of flying off with it, as they do, they would peck her on the cheek and sometimes the lips. She would lift her beautiful head and smile with a radiance that made her look even younger than she was.

238

I looked down the beach and could see new formations of gulls headed for the deck, squealing with excitement as they approached. They dipped low as though making an obeisance to a queen. She would bend and come up with more bits of bread. Some of the gulls strutted about at her feet, snatching a few crumbs here and there, before finding a place on her shoulder. She would stroke them and they would almost sing in their delight.

She looked over at me and smiled.

"They are my dear friends," she said. "I don't know what I would do without them."

It seemed a strange thing to say. But I dismissed it as the exaggeration of a lonely woman's affection for her doting pets. I heard her speak to them softly, in a bell-like voice, as though she was their mother.

"Now go away, children," she said, "and come back later."

After the birds had flown off, she proceeded to make me comfortable, drawing up a chaise lounge and pouring me a glass of freshly minted orange juice.

"I noticed," I said, "how you spoke to them."

"Oh, yes," she said, crossing her shapely legs, "they like that. We have a language of our own. We have a perfect understanding."

"Can you bring the birds back when you like?"

She concentrated for a moment, her eyes closed, and soon overhead there was a covey of screeching sea gulls.

She frowned and they were off again. It was magic. No sultan could have had more obedient slaves. I was ready to believe she could think them into doing whatever she wanted.

I found her interesting. She had a sensuous quality that would take the fancy of any man. It was accentuated somehow by her wide-eyed innocence, the purity of her manner, and a slim, girlish figure that understated her charm. She had a fascinating remoteness.

"I see now," I said, "that you do communicate with animal life."

She laughed merrily, the laugh of a young person so sure of herself, so well-adjusted, that you just felt she was full of kindness and love.

"Your friend must have told you that. He gives me more credit than I deserve."

There didn't seem to be too much of a story. For after you said she could call in the birds at feeding time, by just thinking it, what did you say? There was no air of expectancy here, no thought of suspense. I didn't mind. I liked looking at her, sitting in the soft sun and watching the waves. The salt air had the tang of good wine. It was late in the season and swimmers and surfers had long departed. The beach was deserted. There were no homes nearby, and those I could see in the distance were remote. It was a writer's paradise.

I was lost in my thoughts, and looked up to catch her frown. The noble brow was ruffled for a moment. I followed her gaze down the stretch of beach. I saw a lone figure rounding a bend, moving in our direction. Her brow soon smoothed out but she didn't take her eye off the figure. As the figure drew closer, I could see it was a man. He was dressed in street clothes like myself. He seemed to be a young man, but for his stumbling gait, and the cane he poked along with. He seemed unsure of each step as he picked his way up the beach.

Her eyes had narrowed the least bit. She appeared distracted, even uncomfortable.

"Would you like to go inside?" She gave a slight shiver. "It's chilly this time of the year."

"Oh, no," I said. "I'm quite happy out here. It isn't every day I get a working holiday."

The sea gulls had arrived again out of nowhere. They were fluttering overhead, squealing in their excitement.

She had no eye for the birds. Her gaze was riveted on the young man. He was close enough now so that I could see he was wearing dark glasses. He was counting off his steps with the cane, as if measuring the distance. He stopped in front of the house, and made a turn toward it, using his cane as a guide with each step he took. As his cane rapped against the side of the deck, he stopped and looked up. He called out her name.

"Angela," he cried. "Angela."

There was a plea in his voice. He waited her answer, his head raised, not quite looking at her. I wondered why he hadn't climbed the steps and come onto the deck.

She looked at me for a moment, then said with an air of resignation.

"Yes, Edward."

"May I come up? I have to talk to you. Please."

She looked at the gulls. They had been hovering about, and now were circling low over his head, chattering among themselves.

She gave the birds a second look and shook her head. Her eyes closed, as if she were in rapt concentration.

The birds appeared to hesitate in flight. And then, without another sound, in perfect formation, they flew off down the beach and out to sea. They were soon out of sight.

She sat with her hands folded in her lap, her face serene, like a women in trance. She seemed to have forgotten the young man.

He still waited.

"Angela," he called again.

She opened her eyes, and said in a resigned voice, "Yes, come up, if you like."

He moved with uncertainty, tapping his cane against the steps, groping for a handrail. I realized for the first time, with a sense of shock, that he was blind. Tapping his cane on the steps, he made his way up to the deck. She made no move to help him, and I took my cue from her. He knocked against a deck chair, and edged himself into it, dropping the cane to the floor.

He knew where she was sitting by her voice, and turned toward her.

"I had to see you, Angela," he said. "I humbly ask your forgiveness."

Her face had become a mask. It was still beautiful, but cold and forbidding.

"I have a visitor, Edward."

He sighed. "I'm sorry, Angela. I didn't mean to intrude."

She gave me a pointed glance. I moved down the deck a ways, stretching out on a lounge chair and looking at the ocean. I didn't eavesdrop, but their voices raised from time to time so I couldn't help but get the sense of it.

He spoke with the same pleading note, his words tripping over each other in his anxiety.

"I didn't know what I was doing, Angela. You have to believe me. I don't know what came over me. I had been drinking. I would have died rather than hurt you."

"But you did hurt me." Her voice had a razor's edge. "You destroyed my integrity as a woman. You treated me like a common street girl."

"Forgive me," he cried. "Haven't I suffered enough?"

By this time I had some idea of what had taken place. As I took in the purity of that lovely face, I could understand her anger.

"I forgive you, Edward." Her voice was taut with emotion. "But I cannot forget. I'm sorry."

There was no regret in her voice.

I could sense his despair.

"You were all I thought of in the hospital. They told me I would never see again. That hurt. But what hurt most was that I would never see you again."

Her face was still tight.

"Please go," she said. "There is nothing I can do for you. If my forgiveness is a help you have it." She reached over and touched his hand. "I cannot see you anymore. It brings it all back."

He sat for a moment, his hand trembling, then got up, fumbling with his cane. I couldn't see his expression with his dark glasses, but the droop of his shoulders and his labored breathing told me all I needed to know. She stood aloof, as I moved to help him down the steps. He was no more than 35, and he faced a life without light and color, in the bitterness of his blindness and rejection. I sympathized as I watched him stumble down the beach, his head bowed and his feet lagging. He was no longer measuring his strides with his cane. He was a beaten and broken man.

"What a pity," I said. "How did it happen?"

She didn't appear to have heard me.

She was busy again with the birds. They affectionately pecked at her hands and face, as she called each of them by name. I didn't see how she could tell them apart. They all looked alike to me.

"Weren't you a little hard on him? It must be terrible to be helpless, not able to see for the rest of your life."

Her eyes flashed. I saw a glint of steel which quickly turned to a smile as she fondled the gulls clambering over her, cooing as they begged for food and attention. "These were my only friends. The only ones who cared."

I repeated, thinking again she may not have heard me. "How did it happen?"

Two of the gulls had perched on her shoulders and were playfully pecking at her face. She smiled and cooed to them for a moment, sounding almost like a gull herself. Then gently brushed them away from her eyes. "Now go away, children," she said softly, and they flew off without a sound.

"Yes," she said after a while, "they cared."

Kung Fu

*D*avid Carradine. I knew him as Caine in *Kung Fu*. A mystical figure who appeared out of nowhere to help the oppressed and the helpless. With the power of his mind and his physical presence. He looked pretty much the same in street garb, except for that inscrutable look of his. He had been on the front pages lately, charged with breaking up the Hollywood house of actress Barbara Hershey, the star of *Hoosiers* and other films. And now he was telling me he wanted to rent my vacant house in Malibu. I had moved out recently.

"I'm not a professional house-breaker," David assured me with a smile. "I've never broken up a house I lived in."

"You did a good job from all reports," I said, thinking of how much I had left of myself in this home I built on a bluff overlooking the Pacific Ocean. "You know it's furnished."

"Yes, I know. Plenty of room for Bear."

"Bear?"

"Oh, yes, my 200-pound Newfoundland. He's family. I'll vouch for him. He never broke up a house. You've got three acres. Plenty of room for Bear."

"That's a lot of baggage," I said, "a 200-pounder," thinking of what he could do to a bed or a couch.

"Suppose we put him in the lease," said David. "That makes him responsible."

I laughed, getting to like David more and more.

"You have nothing to worry about," he went on. "We'll protect the place."

We solemnly signed the lease. Landlord and tenants. Bear was to provide a paw print when he was in the mood. I had a few misgivings. But I didn't doubt David would do as he said. After all, wasn't he the silent, forceful minister of justice and fair play?

I had only one admonition. I'd put in a new sprinkler system where I'd planted some fig and avocado trees. I expressed concern about the water pipes being damaged by careless gardeners. "The pipes are just below the surface."

"No problem," said David. We shook hands. He moved in with a lovely young wife and Bear. They were model tenants. The house was in the outer regions of Malibu. Quite a hike to the television studios in Burbank. I had moved closer in myself. So I wasn't surprised when David came to me months later and said he would be taking a house in Malibu miles closer to his studio.

"I'm leaving the place in great shape," he said. "Come by and look it over."

I waited until they had moved out, David, his wife, and Bear. I found the house in good order. The grounds were fine, except for some puzzling tire marks I found on the acreage from the house to the highway. The fruit trees appeared to be flourishing. As did the eucalyptus fringing the property. All seemed well. I was still puzzling over the tire marks, though, when a neighbor stopped by. He saw my puzzled look.

"Yeah," he grinned, "David gave a going-away party. They were wheeling their cars all over the place. Not feeling any pain."

"No sweat," I said. "David promised to take care of the place, to preserve it, and he did. What are a few tire marks?"

Many weeks passed. It was October, a time when the land was dry. Fire season in Malibu. A firestorm started up in the hills and driven by fierce winds headed for the sea. From my present home I saw a huge globe of fire in the sky over my empty house. The very heavens appeared to be ablaze. I stood awed by the towering inferno. But not concerned at that point. For the fire monitors were saying that a Malibu fire had never crossed Pacific Coast Highway. I got in my car and tried driving up the highway to check my house, and was blocked by a sheriff detail. "Nobody can get through. Maybe tomorrow. Everything's burning."

The following day, with little left to burn, they were letting homeowners through. I had some credentials with my old address and was waved on by a deputy. "Good luck."

It was a long ride. I saw charred ruins on every side. I saw my neighbors' homes first. They were closer to the highway. They were all burned to the ground. The owners were staring into the smoking remains. My house was 600 feet from the highway. My vision obscured by thick clouds of smoke. As I drew into the driveway my heart stopped. I couldn't make out the house. A huge house next door with its guest house were smoldering ruins. Edging closer, straining my burning eyes, my mouth dropped. My house was standing untouched. Huge geysers of water were pouring down on the roof and splashing against the walls. A fireman was looking over my shoulder. "You're lucky," he said, "the water pipes must have cracked. The heat split them open. Never saw anything like it."

The trunks of the trees dividing my property from the ruins next door were damp but untouched on my side. On the other side the bark was stripped by the flames. My neighbor, standing in the debris of his house, cried out: "Somebody up there must like you."

How could I tell him about Caine's pledge to protect my house? He would have sent for the man with a net. I sighed and moved on. The fire was over. There was nothing left to burn. It was time to heal. Those hurt most would be helped by those who had suffered least. That's how it was in Malibu.

My newspaper days were long gone, but I stopped by Alice's Restaurant, a landmark on the Malibu pier, for a refresher. As I headed for the bar I heard my name being called. I turned and smiled for the first time in three days. It was David. He was sitting down at a table with his wife, and a flock of Carradines. His brothers. I guess Bear was busy.

"How did it go?" he said.

I gripped his hand.

"You saved my house. Like you promised. Though you didn't know you were doing it."

He smiled. "I didn't do it. I never do it." And with that, his face changed. And he was no longer David Carradine, but the man with the inscrutable look. He stood tall, his shoulders back, his arms crossed. His voice took on a deeper, musical tone. "The Lord works his wonders in strange ways," he said. "All we have to do is ask."

Susan and Marilyn

*I*t was a bit of a jolt to a younger Susan Strasberg when Marilyn moved into the Strasbergs' California home. The two actresses had never been intimate, though Marilyn regarded her mentors Lee and Paula Strasberg as the parents she never had.

As a teenager who had blossomed on Broadway in the *Diary of Anne Frank*, Susan was full of her own needs, eager for the parental attention which she now had to share with Marilyn. She felt hurt, but kept this hurt to herself, loving Marilyn as a sister. "She never knew what it was to have a child's early love. She came to my father and mother, crying, 'Shelter me, feed me, love me,' and they did because they loved her in a strange and special way, as if she had been a child out of some past life experience."

Marilyn gave the younger girl a sketch she had done of herself. She hoped it would help Susan to better understand her. It showed her as a little waif, with one stocking sliding forlornly down to her ankle. "This is how I feel about myself." She smiled wryly. "The original glamour girl."

Susan saw that the star was struggling for an identity of her own, after being cruelly buffeted about as an unwanted child. But there was always that deep-rooted pain from a lack of self-esteem. One night Susan heard a rustle in the hall outside her bedroom. She opened her door to see Marilyn on her hands and knees, dazed by champagne and sleeping pills, crawling on the floor, scratching at the bedroom door of Susan's parents in her desperation. The door opened and Susan ducked back into her room. She wept silently to herself. "I knew then that her need was greater than mine. Just as I knew later that she didn't kill herself. She loved life too much. Even when it hurt most. She was used to pain. You get that way in Hollywood sometimes, where reality and illusion are in constant collision. And you can't tell one from the other."

Football

*B*ecause of my brief fling as a sportswriter, Sonny Werblin, the owner of the New York Jets, thought I was another Knute Rockne. He had been considering a new quarterback and asked me what I thought of George Mira, an outstanding passer for a strong University of Miami team.

"I like him," I said, "he can throw a football 75 yards and hit a watermelon."

"I like him, too," Sonny said. "I want you to have lunch with me and my coach, Weeb Ewbanks. Tell him what you told me."

I found Weeb Ewbanks to be a pleasant man. A good listener with a resolute eye and a square jaw. We hadn't got through the appetizer before Sonny, a high-energy type, turned to me, saying: "Tell Weeb what you think."

I was embarrassed, thinking I wouldn't like to be a coach listening to a rank upstart like myself. But Weeb only smiled and gave me his attention.

"I was telling Sonny what a great arm Mira has and how I thought him a quarterback prospect. He was the key to a great Miami season."

Weeb nodded. "He does have that kind of arm. But he's not

tall enough for the pros. He's barely six feet. We need somebody taller, to look over the heads of the giants on the front line and pick up the field at a glance."

Sonny looked at his coach.

"How tall must this wonder man be? Seven feet? Better he should play basketball."

Ewbanks chuckled. "The fellow I have in mind is tough as nails. He's got an ego that doesn't stop. That's what you need in a quarterback. Supreme confidence. The team feeds off him. This boy's a winner. He's used to winning. He won't be satisfied with anything less."

Sonny had been listening with a show of patience.

"How tall is he?"

"Six foot three or so.

Sonny groused and looked at me. "So there's three inches. Mira can stand on his toes."

I was getting a little curious as to who this wonder boy might be.

"He sounds like a combination of Johnny Unitas and Sammy Baugh."

"Naw," said Sonny, "he's a kid out of the Pennsylvania coal mines. Plays for some southern school."

Weeb Ewbanks' square jaw and resolute eye ended the debate. I hadn't heard from Sonny for a couple of weeks. And then I picked up one of the tabloids and saw that he had come to a decision. He had signed the quarterback out of the coal mines to what was then a record contract. Four hundred thousand dollars. Right out of college. The school was Alabama. And the player? Joe Namath.

It wasn't too long before he had the Jets in the Super Bowl. And announced with a flash of the ego Ewbanks liked in his quarterbacks: "We're going to win it all."

And they did.

I don't remember what happened to Mira.

The Braggart

I didn't like the man. He was brash and bold. I'd had him to my home once, and did what I could to avoid him thereafter. So I was properly surprised when I ran into him on the street, and he started to thank me profusely for doing him a good turn.

I gave him a blank look.

"Oh, it was something you did inadvertently. It was in Norway, Narvik, off the beaten path."

He prided himself on being a world traveler, having a size-able income which a hardworking father had worked himself to death for.

I had meant to move on. But curiosity held me.

"I've never been to Norway," I said.

"I just came back." His face was wreathed with smiles as though the memory lingered. "I met this most beautiful girl. You know how lovely these long-legged Scandinavian blondes can be. We met in Oslo. We were both vacationing. She was friendly but that was all. She lived north, near Narvik. I told her my plans were taking me there. Of course they had been made on the spot."

She had smiled, but she wasn't encouraging.

"Anyway, I hired a car and motored up the coast a day after she left."

My interest was waning. He didn't seem to be going anywhere. And he was a dull fellow besides.

"I gather she didn't invite you to ride with her."

"It was just as well. You know how women are. We may have had a falling out and then I would have never got to see her home."

I gave him a surprised look.

"So she invited you into her home?"

"She took me through her house. It was small but quaint and looked out on the sea. She was an artist and her paintings were all over the place. I don't care much for paintings, but I let her know how much I admired them. She didn't seem impressed."

I would have gone on but he piqued my interest. We had moved off to one side. He flowed on.

"We paused a moment in her bedroom. It was a large room, decorated with her paintings. It had a marvelous ocean view. The furniture was picturesque, what you'd expect in the north country, tables and chairs made of driftwood that had settled on the beaches.

"I admired a night table she had made out of three or four pieces of weathered wood. I noticed three or four books stacked up on a table. I picked up the top one and looked at it. And guess what it was?"

"I'm not good at games," I said, wishing he'd get to the point—my connection with this beautiful unknown.

His eyes rolled. "It was your book, *Yoga, Youth and Reincarnation.* As I was holding it in my hand she said, "'That is my favorite book of all time. It changed my life.'"

He looked at me and I could see he was slightly embarrassed.

"I may have been stretching things," he said with a sly smile. "I told her I was a great friend of yours. I hope you don't mind."

My voice turned cold.

"I don't see that it matters."

"Her attitude immediately changed. She wanted to know all about you. You had gotten her doing yoga and it changed her outlook on life. Made her vibrant and self-confident. Upbeat and optimistic. She asked all kinds of personal questions."

He gave me an apologetic look.

"I wanted to please her. So I made up a few things that I thought would fascinate her. And keep her interested."

"Please go on," I said, needing to know what kind of a buffoon he'd made of himself.

"She was so interested she invited me to dinner. In the evening, when it became dark, she told me I could sleep on the couch if I wanted.

"That's where I slept the first night." He winked in that coarse way of his. "After that we went through the exercises. She wanted me to tell you she does the postures faithfully. We did them together."

His smile was so lascivious, so lewd, I felt like wiping it from his face.

"I stayed three days. They were the pleasantest days of my life. Thanks to you and your book. I can never thank you enough."

I shuddered at the thought.

Customs

I had visited with novelist Taylor Caldwell and her husband in Chapala and in the course of this second visit to Mexico had my first bout with Montezuma's revenge. It was not pleasant. I was uncomfortable and short-tempered, wondering why I'd ever left home.

Outside San Diego, on my return, I was stopped for a routine inquiry and search by U.S. Customs agents. A young, hard-looking Customs inspector asked the usual question:

"What are you bringing back to this country from Mexico?"

"A bottle of Kaopectate, some lomitil pills and a stomach problem."

I started to open my bag.

He stopped me with a wave of his hand.

"One question."

I waited.

"Have you been to Mexico before?"

I nodded. And turned again to open my bag with the clear conscience of the innocent traveler.

Again he stopped me. There was a look of disdain on his lips. "You don't have to open your bag," he said. "You're not bright enough to cheat the government. Move on."

The Good Shepherd

I had stopped off in the small town of Winter Park in central Florida. It was a Saturday night and we were having a late dinner when the lady of the house said, "We'll be going to church in the morning. Would you care to join us?"

She saw me hesitate. I had been thinking of some mid-morning tennis before the sun became a ball of fire.

"There were only seven people in the congregation before the new minister came," she said, "and now there's three services because of the crowds. Doesn't that interest you?"

"What time are the services?"

"Nine, ten and eleven."

We decided on ten. The pastor would have already warmed up and yet not tired of giving the same sermon.

"What does he have that's so special?"

The lady smiled. "You will see."

"Is he more like Billy Graham or Jerry Falwell?"

Her smile broadened. "I thought reporters always went to the source."

We left early to be sure of a seat. I wondered for a moment if there was a contradiction in this prudence. In coming early we were doing some other worshiper out of a seat. It hardly seemed Christian.

The lady frowned.

"They won't suffer. They'll be early for the next service."

She should have been a Jesuit.

The church was Episcopal. It was set back among the trees. There was a pastoral atmosphere. People were already thronging in as we arrived. The pastor priest was standing by the door. It would have been hard to miss him. He was a giant. Six-feet-four, with football shoulders and the red clay of Georgia in his hair, face and mien.

The lady introduced me. He gave my hand a warm clasp, and his deep-set eyes met mine with a smile. "Welcome," he said in a quiet voice, "we are pleased you have come to worship with us." With a few words he had made me at one with him and his flock.

The lady gave me a knowing smile.

There was an air of expectancy in the church. A murmur of excitement as though they were awaiting a great event. I looked around me. The church was consoling and friendly in its simplicity. It had a homey air. There was a loft with the seats set back so you couldn't see the choir. The windows were stained with a splash of color, without austerity. Jesus in his sandals and plain brown robe would have felt he was with friends.

The priest had taken the pulpit. He stood looking out at the congregation. The room was so still you could hear the breathing of your neighbor. I looked at the lady. Her eyes were shining, with a glow that erased the years.

I waited and wondered. There wasn't an empty seat. All eyes were trained on the altar. The priest held a Bible in his hands. His eyes were trained on the loft.

"Now we will hear from those our Lord loved so much."

The sweet voices of the children filled the church. The old

hymn, "Rock of Ages," seemed to take on a new and fuller meaning. The priest stood tall, his eyes never wavering, until the last note faded and died away.

His eyes roved over the congregation. Slowly, ever so slowly, until they settled on me as they had on others. I had a feeling that this man I'd met only moments before had a message for me and me alone.

His voice cut through the sunlight filtering through the stained windows.

"Christ lives," he said, taking in the congregation with a look. "If He were dead, there would be no reason for us to be here today. He lives in our every thought and action. Just as everything we do and say lives in Him and gives Him life. He has never left us."

He opened his Bible, skimming its pages until he came to the pages I'm sure he knew by heart.

"This Jesus says to John, his dearly beloved. A message as true now as it was 2,000 years ago:

"'I lay down my life for the sheep. And other sheep I have, which are not of the fold. Them also I must bring and they shall hear my voice. And there shall be one fold and one shepherd.'"

His voice rose in a paean of triumph. "'I lay down my life, that I might take it again. No man taketh it from me, but I lay it down of myself, and I have the power to take it again.'"

He looked up from his pulpit, and his voice was that of a priest addressing his flock. "Christ is love. When you love, outside yourself, you love Him. And you love yourself. So go in love, as He would have you do."

I saw a light in every eye. They all wanted to love and be loved. I could feel the bond between the people in the church. But as they left the church, the light in many eyes faded. And in a few moments some of the faces were grim, and the horns were honking angrily. In the never-ending rush to get nowhere.

The Producer

Arnold Kopelson called on a Sunday. He was a Hollywood producer with credits like *Platoon* and *The Fugitive*. He was also a lawyer, interested in my novel, *The Judge*. In that novel the main character, as a criminal lawyer, had got off 100 killers. And then as a judge sent off not quite as many killers to the chair, saying, "This killer will never kill again." He made sure of it.

Kopelson didn't waste words. Lawyers don't like talking without a meter going. "I'm going to make your movie," he said. "Can you come in tomorrow and discuss it with my staff?"

He greeted me at the door. He gave me a firm handclasp. And a genial smile. He was a man of average height, with the sparkling eye of a man who liked what he was doing. He introduced me around the conference table to his staff. They were young. And interested.

The meeting began. Kopelson threw out the name of Dustin Hoffman. A good actor with one shortcoming. Too short. We proceeded.

"I think," said Kopelson, "you could use a little more action in the middle. It sags a little." The staff nodded.

"Action?"

"Oh, yes, violence."

"Three people are killed in the first chapter," I said.

I looked around the table. All I saw were blank smiles. I couldn't think of anything more. Movies weren't what I was about.

"I think I know who that judge was," he said.

"It's a novel, a piece of fiction."

"He was a great lawyer before he became a judge," Kopelson went on. "When I was a kid I used to stand and look at his house, hoping to catch a glimpse of him."

"He liked young lawyers," I said. "He kept a special place for them in his courtroom."

Kopelson passed the manuscript around. There were frowns. Capital punishment was a killer in Hollywood. Thousands of people had been murdered in California since the people voted the death penalty. And only a couple of people suffered the fate they had inflicted on the innocent. As my judge said, "Nobody has the guts to pull the switch."

I didn't hear from Kopelson. Not for a while. He was busy plotting another picture, *The Fugitive*. It had a great run. And lots of violence. Beginning. Middle. And end.

I had no qualms. My grandmother told me when I was a kid, "Always march to the beat of your own drum." It was sound advice then. And it still is. Arnold Kopelson did it. And so did I. My own way. Knowing everything happens as it's supposed to.

An Extraordinary Man

Richard McKean was born on January 13, 1926, and died almost 69 years to the hour on January 12, 1995. The cycle of life had come full circle, like an eagle flying back to its place of birth, instinctively returning from whence he came. A return to himself. A return to innocence.

And so a son wrote about his father whose life had been crowned by the love of his five children. His obituary would have said he was the average man his age. A World War II veteran, a Lutheran, a longtime salesman and a man who loved and was beloved by his family.

I knew him well, but not as well as I would have liked. For, as his son Scott indicated, he was very much a private man, kind, warm and gentle, who listened within himself to the beat of a different drum. He was a dreamer, who like so many of his fellow Americans these "ordinary" people who are a nation's strength saw tomorrow's hopes in the resolution of today's travails. He was passionately devoted to the exchange of ideas, a bellwether for his children in the unceasing struggle for amity among all people.

He vested his life in his family and friends, and in God and country, and the life hereafter, the salvation promised by Christ. There were rough spots in his life. He was no Pollyanna, seeing only the bright side. In his last days on earth, shot through with pain, he was still able to sum up, with a smile and an indulgent air, the substance of friendship. Not as some maudlin, unreasoning, clinging imperative, but a joining of hearts and minds with a clear appreciation of the inherent meaning of true love. Inside and outside his family.

The son remembered this legacy of the father's at a fond farewell near the California home where Dick McKean was born. Echoing the father's words which were dinned in the son more than once:

"True friendship can be found only between equals. It cannot spring from either pity, remorse or the desire to protect. It is as tough as whipcord, hard as diamonds, and as fragile as crystal. There is respect in it, the ultimate respect that refuses to tamper with or diminish another's spirit. And yet a cordiality that has no difficulty dispensing sympathy and a helping hand to a friend in distress."

I saw Dick McKean two weeks before his passing. Although in pain he was smiling, trading jokes with a group of young people. Off to one side, marveling at his spirit, I asked how he was getting on.

"Fine," he said, his blue eyes twinkling, "I have a lot to look back on and much to look forward to."

He was a brave man. An "ordinary" man. With an extraordinary way about him. In truth, an extraordinary ordinary man.

The Dream

"One stopoff," he said, as he picked me up at the airport. He was always busy. A brilliant surgeon, who I knew like a brother. I had mentioned I was on my way to Canada to look into the story of a girl who claimed to have lived before.

He nodded without any sign of interest. Keeping his eyes on the road. Down a few miles he came to a stop at a one-story framed building.

As we walked in I saw a room crowded with children's cribs, occupied by the oldest-looking people I had seen in one place. And the most helpless. Some made an effort to stand, leaning against the side of their cribs. Others with wavering voices held out their bony arms.

A middle-aged nurse, with a stenciled smile, came forward. She held out her hand. "What a pleasant surprise, doctor. We weren't expecting you until tomorrow. Your regular day."

"No problem," said the doctor. "I'll be in tomorrow."

He proceeded to make his rounds. Stopping at each crib. He patted some on their heads as if they were children, took the trembling hands of others. He spoke in a kindly voice, saying he would be back. The tired faded eyes lighted up for a moment. Some clutched his hand, until he gently released it.

The gray withered faces and shrunken bodies reminded me of something from Shakespeare. Something about the nature of life. We come into the world without hair, without teeth, with faces wrinkled like a prune and with a gasp of pain. And so we leave it. It made me uncomfortable.

"Not one under 90," he said as we climbed into the car.

I knew Robert Crowley, M.D., well enough to know there was a design in whatever he did.

"Now what was that all about?"

"The American dream," he said, without turning his head. "Longevity."

I knew he had something up his sleeve. He was a sophisticated man. A Park Avenue surgeon in New York, chief of surgery in a mineworkers hospital in the Appalachian poverty belt. And now a clinic in his native Ohio. He had probed the sharp edges of life with a scalpel of the mind. And was an author of repute.

"So what is it all about, doctor?"

He smiled. "Why do you think we're here?"

I had read something as a boy that impressed me. "Do the best you can, with what you have, where you are."

He shook his head.

"So why then are we here?" I said.

"To find out why we're here."

I thought about it. It didn't seem to say very much. "And then what?"

"Do it. Get it done. So you can sleep nights."

I gave him a curious side glance. "When did this bolt of lightning strike?"

"Long before you thought of going up to Canada." His eyes narrowed. As though reaching back in time. "When I was a boy in southern Ohio, on the Kentucky border, there were still a handful around who had fought in the Civil War. Like the people in the nursing home. Going over the battles of Shiloh and Murfreesboro a hundred times. It was no wonder as a boy that I dreamed of the Civil War.

"In this dream I was always the same person. Like Mark Twain in his *Mysterious Stranger*. Always a surgeon in the Confederate army, performing all kinds of wonders. It was the first war with artillery powerful enough to disembowel and eviscerate soldiers of flesh and blood. My dream expanded. I saw myself taking the organs of the still-warm dead, transplanting them to the wounded lying next to them. Grafting live skin from the necks and other areas of bodies to bond together those still living. Some lived, some died. I saved some who would otherwise be dead." It was all a dream. He gave the same help to the wounded of both sides. Blue and gray.

"I had taken the oath back then to minister the lame and the halt indiscriminately even as we do today."

He took his eyes from the road for a moment. "I never mentioned this dream as a boy. I knew I would be ridiculed and laughed at. Nor did I think of it as I grew older, going on to medical school. Then at 20, into World War II, serving with the Army medical corps in the fighting at Anzio and Salerno in Italy. I wandered over the bloody battlefield patching up the disembodied wounded, trying to plug up holes I could put my arm in. Passing out morphine like it was candy to men dying horribly in my arms. Gasping out the names of the living who would soon be mourning them.

"The dead and dying exceeded the living on this battlefield. Their bodies still warm, organs and limbs still alive, the skin still breathing. I was desperate. I had saved no one. I feared for my sanity. My role seemed more that of a coroner or pathologist than a doctor sworn to preserve life.

"It was like a slaughter house. There had been no carnage like it since the Civil War. As that thought came to me, vivid pictures of my boyish dream raced through my mind. I recaptured every surgical dissection and procedure. The shells were whistling overhead but I seemed to have a charmed life. As some wounded responded, my spirits revived. My fatigue left me. I labored with renewed energy."

He was so engrossed he hadn't noticed the man standing over him. "I had just sewn together a GI with great gaping wounds when I noticed this officer. He had been silently watching. He was an elderly man, with gray hair and stooped shoulders. He was the chief of our medical unit. He had a puzzled frown on his face.

"'Where did you learn all this, my boy?' he said, leaning over the wounded soldier, inspecting the way I had grafted the skin from his neck to the face where his nose had been.

"I looked up at him. How could I say I had got it all from a dream? They would have sent me off to the funny farm.

"'I must have read it somewhere,' I said.

"He shook his head. 'I haven't seen anybody do the like since my grandfather died. He was a surgeon with the Confederate forces. He didn't have all the spare parts lying around like you do. But he managed.'"

Crowley took a deep breath. His reliving of Anzio had drained him. I knew of the many whose lives he had benefitted and saved in quieter battlefields. I knew how he suffered with them.

He was a doctor who always had time for a patient, but never for a round of golf. A man who seemed to be doing what he was destined to do. A born doctor. Never rich in worldly goods. So often *forgetting* to send out bills when his patients had little in their closets and less on their shelves.

We were drawing up to his house now. He sighed. "I know

nothing of dreams and what causes them. Nor am I familiar with the influence of racial and genetic memories." A thin smile came to his lips. "I know only one thing. I had a dream. And that dream told me why I was here."

A Fleeting Star

Her name was Diane Varsi. She was 30. Though she looked considerably younger with her delicate coloring and childlike gaze. She was a photographer. Which surprised me. She was better looking than any actress or model. We had been introduced by Laura Huxley, widow of novelist Aldous Huxley, hosting a small party in her Hollywood home.

She seemed shy, a novelty in Hollywood. With the smile of a frightened fawn.

"You look like you should be an actress. Did anyone say you look like a young Garbo?"

She blushed and shook her head. "Oh, they say a lot of things. Don't they?"

It was a quiet get-together, mostly older people. We had a chance to chat. There was a vague familiarity about that lovely profile. And the name. Somewhere back in time. A nagging feeling. And then the ring of a distant bell.

"Weren't you the actress who ran out on Hollywood in the middle of a picture? And led reporters on a merry chase?"

She looked away. I saw a flicker of pain in the deep blue eyes.

269

"Where did you finally turn up?"

A faint smile touched her lips.

"New Hampshire."

"You left a great career."

It had been 10 years. She had made her triumphal debut in *Peyton Place*. The critics had raved. They saw a new star blazing across the Hollywood sky. The studio rushed her into another picture. All seemed to be going well until she took off across the country. There was no explanation.

She seemed to have been swallowed up by the earth. The news hounds were soon off on another scent. She married back East, divorced, and returned only recently with two children. It was all a bad dream. A nightmare she wanted to forget. She could talk about it now. It had happened that long ago.

A frown settled on her brow. "We had come to a scene," her voice tailing off, "that called for someone to push my head into a barrel of water. I had a feeling of dread. I didn't know why. But the last thing I wanted was someone plunging my head into that barrel. I turned to the director. 'I'd rather not do that scene,' I said."

She gave me a wan smile. "How could I say I had a premonition? They would have laughed at me."

Everything on the set stopped. It was a big scene. She was coddled, coaxed and finally stormed at.

"One picture and you're a spoiled star." The director was furious.

Her eyes fell. "I'm afraid."

"Of what? A shallow barrel of water? You can't drown. Just relax. It's only a film."

Yes, just a movie. But she was frightened to death. She was aware of all the eyes on her. Some with indulgence. Others hostile. Contemptuous of this slip of a girl who dared hold up a picture. Who did she think she was?

"All right," she sighed, fighting back her tears.

The set came alive. Lights. Camera. Action. She bowed her head over the barrel. The camera ground away as the heavy's hand pushed her head into the barrel. And kept pushing. For a horrifying moment she caught her breath. And then an agonizing pain shot through her head. She gasped underwater. She thought she was going to faint. Her worst forebodings had come true. A nail sticking up from the bottom of the barrel had lodged in her forehead. Just above the eyes.

She was quickly lifted from the barrel, and taken off, stunned and bleeding. All she wanted was to get away. Fly off somewhere. Anywhere. As fast as she could. She had no thought of anything else.

How must she have felt? Alone, hurt, confused. I was appalled. I wanted to reach across the table and comfort her. It had happened 10 years ago. And the memory lingered, creeping up on her when she least suspected. She sat still now, her face composed, like a Grecian statue.

I looked for the scar. It was only a tiny mark now. Not that noticeable unless you looked for it. Or got under the skin.

"I'm not surprised you took off. Only that you came back," I said.

She managed a smile. "It'll be all right. I'm not making pictures now. I'm only taking them."

A Self-Made Man

Wiliam Penn Patrick was a man of many facets. Lean, tough, handsome. With a quicksilver mind and an engaging eloquence. He owned half a dozen companies. From making cosmetics to expanding the human mind. I had been told he was a reactionary and a bigot but saw nothing of this as we sat chatting in his Tiburon home across the bay from San Francisco.

He looked up when a servant came into the room. And whispered. "A rabbi to see you, sir."

He excused himself. He was gone only a few minutes. He sank back in his chair with a sigh. "I always feel better when I talk to this man. He's got a good word for everyone. Even me."

I laughed. "Yes, I understand you're quite the reactionary, to the right of Ronald Reagan."

"Yes, my reputation precedes and exceeds me. I've been called anti-Semitic. And I'm the main support of a Jewish temple. Anti-Hispanic. And my wife's a Chicano. Anti-Catholic. And my children are raised Catholic. Anti-black. And I employ more black executives than all the companies in the country rolled in one."

He had just given a million dollars to the City of Hope, whose hospital served the sick of all races and religions. He had a dozen other philanthropies which benefitted the down-trodden and underprivileged. He had been a fighter pilot in Korea and got around in a rebuilt P-38 when he wasn't traveling in his seafaring yacht. Yet there was a questing look in his eye that spoke of wider interests.

"How," I smiled, "did you get this reputation? You don't seem like a monster."

"I made one mistake. I went into politics. I was lucky to come out alive. I ran against Ronald Reagan in the California primaries. I supported a ballot affirming a homeowner's right to rent to whoever he pleased. I was immediately dubbed a Fascist. And a few other things, which I wouldn't repeat in range of my children.

"Reagan opposed the proposition. He wanted to be governor, more than I did." And president.

We were on the same wavelength in some things. He had used a passage from a metaphysical book of mine as a company slogan. He knew it by heart.

" 'We ask for strength and God gives us difficulties which make us strong. We plead for courage and God gives us dangers to overcome. We ask for favors and God gives us opportunities.' "

I had almost forgotten the lines.

"And he gave you opportunities?"

"He gave me whatever I have."

This was a side few saw. A man who lived very much within himself. Still keeping involved. Restless, probing, looking beyond the bend in the road. He had taken a course in meditation to expand his horizons. He liked it so much he bought the company. Mind Dynamics. I was doing a book on it. *The Power of Alpha Thinking.*

"It's quite simple," he said. "You take a journey by a process of visualization into the subconscious mind. Ten times more powerful than the conscious mind. The state Thomas Edison was in when he invented the electric light and motion picture camera. A state that sharpens your awareness."

He had read a book I did on reincarnation. It had got him thinking without making a believer of him. "I've been thinking about reincarnation lately. Life seems so short when you think of all the things you want to do." He gave me a quizzical look. "You don't come on one way or the other."

"I was trying to be objective, letting the reader judge for himself."

"You must have an opinion?"

"I think it's plausible. When someone in the subconscious state speaks in alien and ancient tongues they know nothing of consciously, you have to wonder where it comes from."

"So what do you believe?"

"It could be some sort of racial memory. An instinctive thing the animals have. Like the salmon going up the same river to spawn and die. Or remembrance. General Patton picking out an extinct Roman battlefield in the South of France."

His ears pricked up. General Patton, a personification of toughness. Hardly one to spin little fairy tales to feed the ego.

"Patton really believed he had been a Roman general?"

"He wrote about it. And discussed it to some length. Questioning historic accounts of Rome's battle with the Carthage invader.

" 'You must have been there before,' his Italian guide said."

" 'Yes,' he replied, 'a long time ago.' "

We conversed along these lines until it came time for me to catch my plane. He took me to the door. "How about spending a few days at my ranch?" He smiled. "Maybe we could finish our conversation about the subconscious state."

"And reincarnation?"

There was a glint of humor in his eye.

"I've never known anyone who came back. Have you?"

"Only what they tell me."

He was in the prime of life. Only 40. With his best years ahead. "Have a good trip," he said.

His eyes followed me to a waiting car. He waved goodbye. The car drove on. I never saw him again.

I was packing my bag when the call came. One of his executives was on the phone. "Bill's gone," he cried. "Gone. I can't believe it."

I sat still. With the phone in my hand. Rousing myself with an effort.

"How did it happen?"

"He took his plane up this morning. He crashed on the ranch. The plane exploded on hitting the ground. There was nothing left."

He broke off and hung up. I was too stunned to make sense of anything. He was that rare man who made an impact on the life of anyone he touched. I wondered as I thought back whether he'd had any warning or premonition.

I'd never know. Not for sure. For he was a man who was always looking ahead. Making the most of life. Like General Patton.

A Miracle

I received a phone call from little Eddie's parents. The father was a noted physician. The boy, eight years old, was dying. He was in a Santa Monica hospital. The best doctors available had been attending him, and yet nobody could help. His bones were softening and appeared to be diminishing. He had all kinds of tests, yet none of the doctors could diagnose his ailment. They knew what it wasn't. It wasn't cancer. It wasn't osteoporosis. Or anything else they knew about that could invade and destroy a boy's skeletal structure and his life.

"He wants to see you," his mother said. "Could you go to the hospital, then have dinner with us?" They lived in Beverly Hills.

I went directly to the hospital. I hardly recognized the boy. He was a shadow of himself. So thin and slight, it looked like a good wind might blow him away. He was glad to see me. He was distraught, pale and languid, with a look of appeal in his eyes. "Jess," he cried, "please get me out of here. I'll die here."

I put my arm around him and embraced him. Ironically, all I felt was bones. He was wasting away. "Yes," I promised, my heart going out to him. "I will get you out of here if I do nothing else."

From the hospital I went to the boy's home. They had three other children. He was the youngest. I soon found out why they had called. I had written a number of metaphysical books, some dealing with psychic healers. The mother had observed two or three psychic demonstrations that had impressed her. The father, brilliant in his field of medicine, had an M.D.'s conventional outlook. But medically he was at his wit's end. Nothing had worked. The mother did the talking.

"We have tried everything and everyone. But our son keeps getting weaker by the day. Do you know anyone who can help him?"

"One big help," I said, "would be to bring him home. Without knowing what is wrong there is little they can do for him. At least at home he will be with the family he loves and who love him."

The boy was brought home. I mentioned a psychic or two. Without having been told what the problem was, one psychic indicated the boy had a calcium deficiency. He suggested a calcium therapy, which had an initial impulse. But with no lasting effect on the pernicious malady that was taking the boy's life.

"What more can we do?" a desperate mother cried.

"You could try a psychic healer."

The father groaned.

"I have observed several of this man's healings," I put in, "documented by medical records. What can be lost?"

"Yes," said the mother, "we are a medical family. But no antibiotic, no treatment of any sort has helped. No one can even tell us the cause. How then can they cure it?"

She looked at her husband. He shrugged. It would be her decision.

"What is the healer's name?"

"Douglas Johnson. He is a spiritualist minister and coun-selor. He lives in Hollywood."

The mother nodded. "We have nothing else."

I contacted Johnson. I asked if he could come to the house.

"I'll do whatever I can," he said. There was no talk of a fee. Or a donation. Then or later.

The family had just finished an early dinner when Johnson arrived. He looked around the room and smiled. He seemed to harmonize with his surroundings. He was a mild-looking man with rosy cheeks that proclaimed his rural Minnesota background.

The mother asked if the children could witness what he did. "Of course." He gave the three older children a smile. "They have a lot of energy."

The father's eyebrows went up. The skeptical doctor. The man of science. What energy? The skepticism was something Johnson had dealt with over the years.

I looked over at Eddie. His eyes were shining. He loved being the center of attention. He was so frail, so thin, that Johnson easily lifted him onto his lap. They looked at each other. Johnson passed his hand over the boy's head.

He spoke softly. "We are going to get you well."

The boy looked at him. "Are you a doctor?"

"Sort of." Johnson grinned.

The other children laughed. It was better than a movie. And their little brother was the star. Sort of. Johnson now held his right hand over Eddie's head. He had eyes only for the boy. No one else existed.

He started to speak, in a penetrating voice. I sensed the heat emanating from his hand across the room. I could see the other children had felt it as well.

"I feel warm," the boy said, peering up at Johnson.

"That's good," said Johnson. "You are being healed in God's name. I am only the instrument. You are being healed by a universal force, which is God's hand at work."

He looked around the room. He could see everyone was caught up in the drama of the occasion. They were a Christian family, aware of Christ's miracles.

"Jesus said," Johnson went on, as the little boy's eyes widened, "that where two or more are gathered, the sick and the lame can be healed."

His eyes fell now on the boy's face and the young eyes that were already glowing. He gave him a little embrace.

"The healing is now in effect," he said. "You will get stronger every day. And in six weeks you will be strong enough to run a race and win it."

The session was over.

The boy did run that race and win it. And now as a young doctor himself he was winning a different sort of race every day. Healing and helping people in his own way a doctor's way. But always remembering. He sent me a message from abroad only two years ago saying he would always be grateful for my saving his life. When, of course, it was Johnson and the good Lord who had done it.

An Encore

The boy Douglas Johnson healed grew up to be a doctor. And a very good one. People flocked to see him. He was an excellent surgeon, a specialist in ailments of the throat and chest. He was patient and skilled and above all he was caring. He never forgot the days when his life hung in the balance, nor the man who tipped the scales for him, though their paths seldom crossed. The young doctor's name grew, and quite often the sick came to him when they couldn't get help elsewhere. Invariably, he found a way to help them. One day a patient, who was also a friend, came to him. He was a young man, like the doctor, and his life, too, hung in the balance. Two years earlier he had a malignant cancer which went into remission with radiation and chemotherapy. But now the cancer had returned, lodging in his lung. The surgeons told him he would require immediate surgery to rid himself of the tumor. They had put him down for surgery in two weeks. He sensed that his chances were not all that good.

He talked it over with the physician who was his friend. Who felt there was little he could do for the friend who had come to him in desperation. He thought a while, his mind traveling back to the days when he himself clung to life by a slender strand. And with a start he thought, "Why not?" He picked up the phone and made a call.

"Do you think Douglas Johnson would help a friend I cannot help? He has a deadly cancer."

I was not surprised by his call, though there was a certain irony in it. "He could try," I said, "it worked for you."

Johnson responded. A meeting was arranged. The young physician stood by. The patient was depressed and confused. He had been on an emotional rollercoaster, his spirits soaring when he was apparently cured, then slumping when the dread disease returned. He knew nothing about psychics. It all seemed a little off the wall. But he had nothing to lose, he told himself. He could always get on with the surgery if this thing didn't work. That's how he thought about it.

Johnson greeted him with a smile and a pat on the shoulder. Johnson was of medium height, slight, with rosy cheeks. From Minnesota originally, of Swedish extraction. So soft-spoken he had to make an effort to be heard. The first session took an hour. "Make up your mind you are going to be healed," Johnson said, "that's half the battle."

As Johnson's hands passed over the young man he could feel the heat deep into his shoulders and chest. It seemed to have an energy of its own. The problems of the day became distant and he had an overwhelming feeling of wholeness. Of being at one with himself. A feeling, too, of exaltation, as if he was being lifted into the heavens. His illness was forgotten.

Johnson embraced him when it was over. "I think it went well. You were totally receptive and at ease."

Next came the surgeons, two weeks later. X rays and tests, preliminary to surgery, were taken. Nothing had been said about a psychic healing. The X rays and tests revealed that the cancer cells in the lung had died. And the tumor had shrunk. The surgery was postponed. There were two more sessions with Johnson. The tumor disappeared. All in three weeks.

Johnson was his usual modest self. "I was only a channel," he said. "The healing vibrations were in the atmosphere, and Spirit, the God within us, did the rest."

As it had before with the small boy who grew up to be a giving doctor.

The Bishop

*T*he bishop would have been an unusual man if he had never talked to a son who was dead. He had been a lawyer and a Catholic, changing both his faith and his calling. He was a controversial figure in his Episcopal church, largely through his outspokenness. He had the same doubts many clergymen had about church doctrine and immortality. He spoke and wrote about them. That was the unforgivable sin.

He was already charged with heresy by his brother bishops. What would they think of a disciple of Christ who had questioned the hereafter and was now flirting with it?

He had stirred an unseemly furor by presumably communicating with his son in a séance on television, and had then withdrawn from the public eye. I was reading about it when an old editor of mine called from the Big Apple.

"I imagine you've heard about the bishop by this time."

"It's all over the place."

"It's wacky. But it's news like everything he does. I'd like you to see what you can do with him. He won't talk to anybody."

"Why should he talk to me?"

He laughed. "You're into that stuff. Birds of a feather, you know."

I considered a moment. He was right. I was interested.

I had no reason to believe the bishop would see me when he wasn't seeing anybody else. But I picked up the phone I had just put down, and called the Think Tank. A study center in Santa Barbara for the world's great scholars, trading ideas in the fields they knew best. The bishop's was theology.

The detached voice of a secretary said:

"I will give Bishop Pike your message."

I left my name and phone number, thinking that would be the end of it. Toward the close of day, the phone rang and the detached voice announced, "Bishop Pike returning your call."

He was on the line, friendly and effusive. I thought for a moment he had me confused with somebody else. But not for long.

"I owe you a debt," he said, "a book of yours on prophecy changed my thinking. Here I was a bishop of a Christian church, not realizing there were people today repeating the miracles Jesus had performed 2,000 years ago. I understood better his miracles, through seeing what others had done as He said they could with faith in the Father. A faith which enabled Him to heal the sick and to know the dead still lived."

The one phrase turned over in my head as I drove up the California coast. "To know the dead still lived." It told me something of his thinking.

It was a pleasant drive. Little more than an hour. He was in conference when I arrived. He came out immediately. He was not quite what I had expected. His physical appearance wasn't at all impressive. He was of middle height, middle-aged, with the face of a country parson. But when he spoke, he became electric. His face lit up, his voice soared. He looked at you directly, and you had the feeling you were the only person in the world right then. He smiled frequently. You would never have known he had suffered a grievous loss.

He gave me a seat overlooking the mountains and the sea, and served refreshments as we talked. I thought it important to understand the relationship between father and son, and the circumstances of the boy's death. The boy was only 20 when he took his life. He had lived most of his years in the shadow of his famous father. He was not an achiever. He had trouble with his studies, trouble with drugs. Trouble finding himself. They had spent the last few months together in England, the father taking a teaching sabbatical at Cambridge, the son making up grades at a small college nearby. They had traveled to the Holy Land. In the Negev desert they had felt a spiritual bond which seemed to fore-shadow a new awakening between them. The memories of the land clung to them, bringing them close to the Son of Man and the tiny band who traveled the glory road with Him. They felt themselves in the presence of the Almighty who had led His people out of slavery into the land of promise. They felt God speaking to them, and their hearts sang of the love they felt in that moment for each other. They embraced.

"I felt closer to my son that day than ever before. It was as if we understood each other for the first time, and our spirits were joined for all time."

I saw the suspicion of a tear in his eye.

"Some day I will return to the Negev, and experience that closeness again. We will never be far apart."

They had shared the father's flat in England. Their books and papers and other belongings were mingled in the various rooms and closets. On returning from Israel, the son packed up his things and made ready to go back to the States. The father had a good feeling about Jim, the prodigal son named after him. The boy seemed more cheerful than the father could remember.

"He was still the young iconoclast, questioning the integrity of his elders, thinking, by and large, like so many his age, that it was a greedy heartless world. I tried to show him another side of humanity, people who cared about people. It was up to him and his generation to create a better world for themselves and their children. He seemed satisfied, somewhat reassured. We embraced and spoke of our love for each other. I felt good about him. I felt he was going to be all right. I had been concerned about drugs. He said he realized how much they had hurt him."

A few days later, as he was about to deliver a lecture, a colleague took the bishop aside. He knew immediately something was wrong. Icy fingers clutching at his heart told him it had to do with his son. He had taken his life in a lonely hotel room in the States. The bishop was devastated. In his grief he relived every moment with his son. What could he have done different? He prayed and he wept. He searched into his soul for the answer. He found none. To say it was God's will gave him no consolation. There was no greater sorrow than a parent mourning a lost child.

He hastened back to California and joined with his family in the last rites for the son. They tossed the boy's ashes in the bay, within sight of the Golden Gate Bridge, while the father was still asking why. Why had he done it? Why hadn't he talked about it? It would have helped to know what had gone through his mind those last tortured hours.

Thoughts churned around in his head. Good memories and bad. And always he came back to that day in the desert near Beersheba, where father and son looked deep into each other and knew they were bound for the ages.

With all of the regrets and the pain, there was no sorrow in his voice. I found this puzzling at the time, for I did not know what he was thinking.

He returned to England within the week to the apartment they had shared. Every place he looked there were mementos of the boy. He picked up the postcards Jim had bought in Israel and not sent, souvenirs of their stay in the Holy Land. He turned open a book or two they had glanced through, and wistfully eyed the family pictures the boy had snapped. He felt the boy's presence, and looked around fitfully, then chided himself for imagining things. He had to get a hold on himself. He had heard that a spirit remained earthbound for a while after death because of the violent end that was chosen. He had no belief in spirits. His legally trained mind had always required evidence of an afterlife. Though he believed in Christ's resurrection, he had never been entirely convinced of the continuity of life. He wanted to believe, never more than now.

So far there had been little in his story different from the reactions of others who had lost someone dear to them. I was about to broach his sittings with spiritualists when he asked with a quizzical smile:

"Do you believe in poltergeists?"

I understood them to be playful spirits, which returned after death to convey a message from the other side.

"I've never understood," I said, "how a spirit could move a piano, in its etheric state, when it couldn't do it in the flesh."

"In other words you don't believe in spirits. Well, neither did I."

"But you do now."

I was not too surprised. Why else would he have consulted a medium?

"I have to believe my own eyes. Particularly, when two of my colleagues shared my experience."

Strange things began to happen shortly after he got back to England. Two of his books, left on the floor of his bedroom, reappeared, as if by magic, hours later on his dresser. They were books with a special relevance for him at this time. One was the Bible, the other on suicide and the soul. This was only one of many puzzling diversions to occur while he was away from his apartment for a few hours. Snapshots of the trip to Israel, edged into the dresser mirror, were found in the living room. A clock on the wall was stopped at 8:19, the precise time of his son's death. Two postcards, found on the floor, were positioned at the same 8:19 angle as the hands of the clock. Some windows were flung open, others closed, drawers were emptied, safety pins opened, closets ransacked. It looked like somebody had swept through the place. He didn't know what to make of it. He was thoroughly confused.

I saw nothing evidential about any of this except for the clock. And even this could have been arranged by a human hand. A maid, a janitor, a friend could have come by in his absence. All they needed was a key.

"Could it have been your maid?"

He had expected the question.

"There was no maid on this day, and no janitor."

"Friends?"

Two aides supported his story. "The three of us, together, watched a silver hairbrush move as if by itself, sliding against gravity up a slanting closet shelf. One caught the brush just before it hit the floor."

One aide, a young woman, found her bangs had been snipped off her forehead while she slept. The bishop thought this more significant than I did. "I remembered," the bishop said, "that my son often teased her about cutting her bangs."

Why couldn't she have done it? To let a grieving father think it was the son he missed.

"Are you suggesting that your son's spirit visited the apartment and playfully trimmed the girl's hair?"

"At that point I didn't know what to believe. But my mind was open. I had no other explanation of what had moved about the articles I mentioned."

It seemed to me that anybody who died and came back should have better things to do than give somebody a haircut.

"Why not just tell you he is here?"

The bishop smiled.

"Maybe that's what he did."

There was more, some of it disconcerting. An aide, meaning to waken the bishop, had found him sitting up in bed, talking in his sleep, in language so unlike him that she was stunned. He was saying that people were uncaring, indifferent, moved by greed and self-interest, thinking only of themselves. Life was mean and tawdry, hardly worth the living.

She spoke to him about it. He was startled. "The words she attributed to me," he said, "were pretty much the way my son saw things. It was as though he was talking."

It sounded like a hallucination, but I had no wish to dash any hopes he had of his son's survival.

"Was it your feeling that your son's spirit took over your voice?" I tried to keep the skepticism out of my voice.

"I didn't know what to think. Something was going on and I wanted to know what."

He discussed the experience with an English colleague, knowing that English churchmen were more involved in the metaphysical. The colleague suggested he consult a London medium, Ena Twigg. "She has some interesting contacts on the other side," he said.

The bishop laughed to himself.

"Here I was being damned by my brother bishops for not believing enough, and now they would damn me for believing too much."

He didn't know what to expect of a spiritualist. He had never attended a séance. Ena Twigg soon put him at ease. She was a motherly looking woman with a gentle voice. Her sitting room was plainly furnished. There were no flashing lights, no velvet drapes, no dramatics. She knew nothing of his story. The spirit would have to identify himself. It would get no help from her.

After a brief delay she began to speak. The spirit was speaking through her. He did not identify himself. His words were for the bishop. They gave him a chill. It was obvious who he must be.

He spoke of taking his life. "My nerves were jumpy from the drugs. I brooded over my failures. I know now they were less than I thought. I was confused, lonely. It was an impulse of the moment. I'm sorry."

With a start, the bishop heard Ena Twigg go on, clarifying the poltergeist activity, as though it was the son still speaking. "I wanted you to feel my presence. I came to your rooms. I moved the books and the postcards. I set the clock. And I spoke to you. You were in your bedroom, just coming out of your sleep."

This was the gist of it. The bishop mulled it over in his befuddled mind. His objective mind told him he could be going through an exercise of wishful thinking. But, still, where was it all coming from? What Ena Twigg had said was known only to him. He had not given any of the details to his English colleague. His curiosity was stimulated, not only by the desire for contact with his son but by his fascination with the prospects of survival.

There was some publicity about the sitting in England. Returning to the States, he was besieged by serious-minded people who wanted to know more about it. He went on a television talk show in Canada with the noted medium, Arthur

Ford, not knowing it would turn into a séance. The televised sitting repeated the information already given. There was an admonition by the son to fight the heresy charges brought by the church.

"They will be dropped."

And so they were.

I didn't know what to make of it. I wasn't sure the bishop did. Whatever he chose to believe, there had to be some lingering doubt in so orderly a mind. Which may have accounted for his eagerness to return to the Holy Land, and the trackless desert he had visited with his son.

In his heart, I could see, he was already on his way. I hoped he would find what he was looking for. As he spoke of the Negev he looked youthful, almost boyish. I never saw him again, but I remember him smiling, his eyes turned to the East.

As he wished, he made his journey back to Israel, crossing into the Negev where he had rejoiced in his spiritual reunion with his son.

In the desert where their souls had joined, his car inexplicably stalled. He went off on foot looking for help. His body was found days later in the desert wasteland. They said the desert had taken his life. I'm not sure. It may have been something else, something to do with destiny. Something he had felt when he and the son he loved looked into each other's souls.

I have wondered whether the bishop and Jim found their peace in a world where nobody grows older and the dead communicate with the living. I like to think of him one day waving a hand in greeting and saying with a smile, "I told you so. Why didn't you believe me?"

Epilogue

Among the memories that lingered and grew in time was that of the immigrant Italian bootblack, who shined shoes on a Manhattan ferry. His price was 50 cents. Spelled out on a placard around his neck. I was so pleased by the result I gave him a dollar and told him to keep the change.

He scowled, "My price is 50 cents."

He hobbled away, bent with years, stopping with his shoeshine box every now and then, his bare head exposed to the cold wind that whistled across the river.

As I got along in life, meeting people of all stripes, his image became an indelible medallion of independence and merit. A meeting as fresh in my mind today as it was then.

I remember the Old One, the Patriarch, sitting so proudly in the Inaugural box, as I remember my tears as a solemn procession rolled down Pennsylvania Avenue bearing a fallen leader who personified vibrant youth and courage to millions of his countrymen. Tears for what he was, and for what he wasn't. Tears for the promise unfulfilled. The opportunities missed. Tears for the charm and the quick wit, the ready sympathy for the poor and the powerless. Tears most of all for what might have been. The simple coffin draped with the flag making a hollow memory of greatness and fame.

My thoughts turned to the Old One, the father so proud of the achievement of the son who realized the father's own fondest dream. I remembered the letter the Old One sent me after his son's election, telling me of his plans to discontinue his attacks on Lyndon Johnson, the new vice president.

"It would not be appropriate," he wrote, "now that I am the father of the president."

I wondered what he thought then, in his grief, two sons tragically lost, in war and in peace. And Lyndon Johnson becoming president over the body of his dead son. I wondered if he found comfort in what the Good Book had to say, "Vanity of vanities, saith the preacher, all is vanity."

I often wondered how my life might have gone had I responded to Clark Gable's invitation to visit him in California. Publishers were clamoring for his life story and I could have collaborated. It was the same year I was beginning to show interest in the metaphysical and I might never have gone on to do the research I did. My only regret, however, was that I didn't get to better know this unusual man for whom I had so strong an affinity. Yet something lasting did come of our meeting. I fell in love with California and eventually moved there. I had been inspired for years by Nelson Eddy's recording of *The Hills of Home*. I found those hills in Malibu, Malibu by the sea. Something that might never have happened had it not been for my meeting with the King—Clark Gable.